SIR EDMUND HILLARY AND TENZING NORGAY

OYSTER PERPETUAL EXPLORER

Team Principals, Susie and Toto Wolff, watching their future generation race ahead.

Are we doing our best for future generations?

Will they be prepared?

How can we give them the right start?

Future generations are our legacy to the world. So we want them to be well-equipped for the challenges ahead. But in these changing times, what skills will they require? And how much will we need to set aside? Together, we can help give them the best chance of success. For today and tomorrows to come.

For some of life's questions, you're not alone. Together we can find an answer.

THE 7

BMW 745e xDrive:
Fuel consumption in l/100 km (combined): 2.2–2.1
Energy consumption in kWh/100 km (combined): 15.5–15.1
CO_2 emissions in g/km (combined): 51–48

BAYERISCHE MOTOREN WERKE

WARNING: THE FOLLOWING MAGAZINE MAY CHALLENGE PREVAILING OPINION.

It's perhaps fitting that I'm writing this from the last major city that will ring in 2020. Yes, dear reader, I'm hard at work in Honolulu as we send THE FORECAST to press and I'm very much looking forward to the year ahead. It's also fitting that I'm writing this from one of the outermost time zones because something rather odd happens when you're this far behind the global centres of decision making: you soon realise there's a certain pleasure that comes with being a little off the global conversation. When you're 19 hours behind Tokyo, 10 behind London and five adrift of New York, a lot of decisions and discussions have happened while you're either fast asleep or tucking into your lightly grilled *opakapaka* (think of it as a pink snapper). Although there's a thrill that comes with being at the centre of the chatter and breaking news, there's also a great relief at being able to absorb, digest and analyse when geography leaves you far from the world's major editorial hubs.

For the past year there has been considerable discussion across our own editorial floor about the luxury that comes from stepping outside the English-language news cycle and not relying on three or four major New York/London-based news outlets that are stuck on the same five stories, plus another three or four with themes that play a dangerous game of click-bait dressed up as righteous campaigning. If you're blessed with a command of a second or third language then it's easy to obtain a broader world view by dipping into the pages of Norway's *Aftenposten*, France's *Les Echos* and Brazil's *Folha da São Paulo*, or tuning into a cultural debate on Austria's ORF.

If your German or Portuguese isn't fully polished, you needn't feel left out. Mr Google's translate function does a decent to occasionally excellent job of getting the point across by swapping an opinion piece or weighty bit of reportage into your language of choice.

For sure, a bit of nuance is lost across 1,800 words of analysis on modern Poland and there's a lack of beauty in the prose of a 3,500-word interview in *Die Zeit*. But, at the very least, you'll walk away with a perspective that is far away from what's being trotted out as a "world view" by the English-language media.

Spend a bit of time in the pages of Spanish, French, Mexican, German and Swiss dailies and you'll soon realise that things aren't quite as straightforward as the English-language powerhouses would have us believe. And thank heavens. Whereas less popular points of view have been shut out in many English-language media outlets, controversial opinions can still find a full page in a very respectable outlet elsewhere.

Before I touched down at my base in the mid-Pacific, MONOCLE hosted a small but punchy cities conference in Chengdu in early November. Over a lively hotpot dinner with various delegates (most of them British, Australian and Dutch) there was a point when the volume of conversation lowered and my dinner guests started glancing over their shoulders and speaking into their napkins – not because of the volcanic Sichuan peppers spiking every mouthful but because they had something potentially potent to say. It was at this point that I was reminded how stifled conversations have become in the English-speaking world and how terrified many people are of putting a foot wrong by being culturally insensitive or not being abreast of the latest "no-go" topics – and having a point of view that's not part of the mainstream.

By now you might be familiar with this parallel global conversation that is happening across dinner tables, in quiet corners of dimly lit bars, between the seats of heavily upholstered cars and anywhere else that people find themselves out of earshot and among those they can trust. Only in these safe spaces can differing views be presented, the seemingly absurd be

The MONOCLE
FORECAST

We need to turn down the shouting and listen to other people's ideas – even if they challenge our Anglo-Saxon views

MIN

questioned or the clearly ridiculous dismissed. We like to think that all these media platforms allow for a grand, global discussion but it couldn't be further from the truth. Instead of providing a variety of views and allowing for intelligent debate, too many English-language news outlets have shifted to the default stance of being do-good campaigners rather than taking the balanced position of being questioning news outlets.

As MONOCLE develops its story line-up for 2020, we want to ensure that we present a variety of views and opinions that are well removed from the narrow agenda being driven by others. Ours may not be the most popular take on the world but that's just the way we want it. We're here to question, to challenge and, more importantly, to present perspectives that fail to find space in other outlets.

I welcome your thoughts on the above; you can get in touch with me at *tb@monocle.com*. In the meantime, thank you for all your feedback and support during the course of 2019. I can assure you that it encourages our fresh take on global affairs, business, culture and design – and all the other elements that define THE FORECAST and MONOCLE. Cheers. — (M)

CONTENTS.

Affairs. *Moving capitals p28 — 35*

Culture. *Budapest: film city p99 — 103*

The MONOCLE
FORECAST

CHAMPAGNE

LA GRANDE DAME

Veuve Clicquot

Food and travel. *Bouillons p164 — 169*

Travel. *Hotel Halekulani Okinawa p179 — 181*

Fashion. *Benchmark retailers p141 — 146*

KEY TO WRITERS

(MKA) Mikaela Aitken. (LA) Liam Aldous. (HAN) Hamish Anderson. (AB) Aarti Betigeri. (MB) Michael Booth. (RB) Robert Bound. (PB) Petri Burtsov. (IC) Ivan Carvalho. (ALC) Alice Cavanagh. (JCH) James Chambers. (ABC) Annabelle Chapman. (GDE) Gabriele Dellisanti. (LE) Lucinda Elliott. (JAF) Josh Fehnert. (AAF) Audrey Fiodorenko. (NSG) Nolan Giles. (LHO) Louis Harnett O'Meara. (WK) Will Kitchens. (AKO) Alexei Korolyov. (TL) Tomos Lewis. (GSL) Gaia Lutz. (AMG) Ann Marie Gardner. (CMG) Charlotte McDonald-Gibson. (NM) Nic Monisse. (SMW) Sorrel Moseley-Williams. (AM) Andrew Mueller. (DMP) David Plaisant. (NPO) Naomi Potter. (LLP) Lyndee Prickitt. (CCR) Carlota Rebelo. (MSS) Marie-Sophie Schwarzer. (CSM) Clarissa Sebag Montefiore. (CST) Chloe Stead. (EJS) Ed Stocker. (KTS) Karina Tsui. (HU) Hester Underhill. (AW) Annick Weber. (JWE) Julia Webster. (FW) Fiona Wilson. (SZ) Sonia Zhuravlyova. (ZZ) Zayana Zulkiflee.

TO DO SOMETHING COOL

ONE OF **7974 073** REASONS TO FLY

FINNAIR

MAGAZINE. RADIO.
ONLINE. FILM.

EDITORIAL

Tyler Brûlé. Editor in Chief & Chairman… *tb@monocle.com*
Andrew Tuck. Editor… *at@monocle.com*
Richard Spencer Powell. Creative Director… *rsp@monocle.com*
Jacqueline Deacon. Production Director… *jd@monocle.com*
Lewis Huxley. Chief Sub Editor… *lh@monocle.com*
Matthew Beaman. Photography Director… *mpb@monocle.com*
Robert Bound. Senior Editor… *rb@monocle.com*
Josh Fehnert. Executive Editor… *jaf@monocle.com*
Megan Gibson. Foreign Editor
Nolan Giles. Design Editor… *nsg@monocle.com*
Thomas Reynolds. Managing Editor… *tr@monocle.com*
Chiara Rimella. Culture Editor… *chr@monocle.com*
Marie-Sophie Schwarzer. Travel & Inventory Editor…
mss@monocle.com
Sophie Grove. Senior Correspondent
Daphné Hézard. Fashion Director… *dhz@monocle.com*
Jamie Waters. Fashion Editor… *jsw@monocle.com*
Venetia Rainey. Business Editor… *vr@monocle.com*
Christopher Cermak. Affairs Editor… *cc@monocle.com*
Kyoko Tamoto. Fashion Markets Editor… *kt@monocle.com*
Louis Harnett O'Meara. Researcher… *lho@monocle.com*
Nic Monisse. Researcher… *nm@monocle.com*

DESIGN

Yoshitsugu Takagi. Design Director… *yt@monocle.com*
Sam Brogan. Associate Art Director… *sbr@monocle.com*
Shin Miura. Deputy Photo Editor… *smi@monocle.com*
Maria Hamer. Senior Designer… *mjh@monocle.com*
Pedro Beça. Product Designer… *pb@monocle.com*
Victoria Cagol. Assistant Photo Editor… *vc@monocle.com*
Giulia Tugnoli. Junior Designer… *gt@monocle.com*

BUREAUX

Fiona Wilson. Bureau Chief Asia (TOKYO)… *fw@monocle.com*
Kenji Hall. Asia Editor at Large (TOKYO)… *kh@monocle.com*
Junichi Toyofuku. Associate Bureau Chief (TOKYO)… *jt@monocle.com*
James Chambers. Bureau Chief (HONG KONG)… *jch@monocle.com*
Karina Tsui. Researcher (HONG KONG)… *kts@monocle.com*
Ed Stocker. Americas Editor at Large (NEW YORK)… *ejs@monocle.com*
Tomos Lewis. Bureau Chief (TORONTO)… *tl@monocle.com*
Will Kitchens. Researcher (TORONTO)… *wk@monocle.com*
Carlo Silberschmidt. Production Coordinator (ZÜRICH)… *cs@monocle.com*
Carlota Rebelo. Acting Bureau Chief (LOS ANGELES)… *cr@monocle.com*

SUB EDITING

Rachel Kurzfield. Deputy Chief Sub Editor
Nick Mee. Acting Deputy Chief Sub Editor… *njm@monocle.com*
Sonia Zhuravlyova. Sub Editor… *sz@monocle.com*
Rosie Prata. Editor, Advertorials… *rp@monocle.com*

ONLINE

Rogerio Mota. Senior Digital Designer… *rmm@monocle.com*
Joe Gwynn. Senior Web Developer… *jg@monocle.com*
Bill Whitehouse. Digital Producer… *bw@monocle.com*
Rebecca Ricci. Digital Assistant… *rr@monocle.com*

FILM

Helena Kardová. Senior Producer… *hk@monocle.com*

BOOKS

Joe Pickard. Editor… *jp@monocle.com*
Chloë Ashby. Associate Editor… *ca@monocle.com*
Hester Underhill. Assistant Editor… *hu@monocle.com*

MONOCLE 24 RADIO

Tom Edwards. Executive Producer… *te@monocle.com*
Markus Hippi. Senior Producer/Presenter… *mh@monocle.com*
Holly Fisher. Senior Producer… *hf@monocle.com*
Rhys James. Senior News Producer… *rj@monocle.com*
Daniel Bach. Producer/Presenter… *db@monocle.com*
Ben Rylan. Producer/Presenter… *br@monocle.com*
Carlota Rebelo. Producer… *cr@monocle.com*
Bill Leuty. Producer… *bl@monocle.com*
Fernando Augusto Pacheco. Producer and Culture Correspondent…
fp@monocle.com
Tom Hall. Associate Producer… *th@monocle.com*
Augustin Macellari. Associate Producer… *ama@monocle.com*
Joleen Goffin. Associate Producer… *jog@monocle.com*
Paige Reynolds. Associate Producer… *pbr@monocle.com*
Sam Impey. Head of Production… *sji@monocle.com*
Christy Evans. Studio Manager… *ce@monocle.com*
David Stevens. Studio Manager… *djs@monocle.com*
Mae-Li Evans. Studio Manager… *me@monocle.com*
Nora Hoel. Studio Manager… *nh@monocle.com*

CORRESPONDENTS

Mikaela Aitken (BRISBANE)… *mka@monocle.com*
Liam Aldous (MADRID)… *la@monocle.com*
Justin Bergman (MELBOURNE)… *jb@monocle.com*
Lars Bevanger (OSLO)… *lab@monocle.com*
Michael Booth (COPENHAGEN)… *mb@monocle.com*
Kimberly Bradley (BERLIN)… *kab@monocle.com*
Nick Brown (DEFENCE)… *nb@monocle.com*
Tom Burges Watson (PARIS)… *tbw@monocle.com*
Petri Burtsov (HELSINKI)… *pbu@monocle.com*
Ivan Carvalho (MILAN)… *ic@monocle.com*
Annabelle Chapman (WARSAW)… *abc@monocle.com*
Guy De Launey (LJUBLJANA)… *gdl@monocle.com*
Zach Dundas (PORTLAND, OREGON)… *zd@monocle.com*
Alex Duval Smith (ABIDJAN)… *ads@monocle.com*
Lucinda Elliott (LATIN AMERICA AFFAIRS)… *le@monocle.com*
Christopher Frey (TORONTO)… *cf@monocle.com*
Sasha Issenberg (WASHINGTON)… *si@monocle.com*
Daphne Karnezis (ATHENS)… *dk@monocle.com*
Alexei Korolyov (VIENNA, RADIO)… *ako@monocle.com*
Gabriel Leigh (TRANSPORT)… *gl@monocle.com*
Liv Lewitschnik (STOCKHOLM)… *ll@monocle.com*
Alexander Matthews (JOHANNESBURG)… *agm@monocle.com*
Tristan McConnell (NAIROBI)… *tmc@monocle.com*
Charlotte McDonald-Gibson (THE HAGUE)… *cmg@monocle.com*
Anastasia Moloney (BOGOTÁ)… *anm@monocle.com*
Ricardo Moreno (SÃO PAULO)… *rm@monocle.com*
David Plaisant (ROME)… *dmp@monocle.com*
Lizzie Porter (BEIRUT)… *lpo@monocle.com*
Gwen Robinson (BANGKOK)… *gr@monocle.com*
Sarah Rowland (SOUTHERN STATES, USA)… *sr@monocle.com*
Laura Rysman (CENTRAL ITALY)… *lr@monocle.com*
Janek Schmidt (MUNICH)… *js@monocle.com*
Clarissa Sebag-Montefiore (SYDNEY)… *csm@monocle.com*
Jason Strother (SEOUL)… *jws@monocle.com*
Annick Weber (LUXEMBOURG)… *aw@monocle.com*

INTERNS

**Josh Greenblatt, Will Higginbotham, Nicholas Toomey,
Samraweet Yohannes**

GEORG JENSEN

ESTABLISHED 1904

THE GIFT
OF GIVING

The things we share, the moments we create, the gifts we give - we are each given to inspire.
This season, it is time to cherish the ones you love. Time to show just how much you care. It's time
to enjoy the gift of giving.

WWW.GEORGJENSEN.COM

COPENHAGEN · STOCKHOLM · LONDON · NEW YORK · SYDNEY · TOKYO · MUNICH · SINGAPORE · TAIPEI

PUBLISHING. MARKETING.
DISTRIBUTION. RETAIL.

PUBLISHING
Anders Braso. Publisher… *ab@monocle.com*
Luke Courtier. Head of Creative Solutions… *lc@monocle.com*
Nicolas Yllera. Advertising Director – Luxury & Global Affairs… *ny@monocle.com*
Sabrina Toldt-Zimmerhofer. Account Director… *stz@monocle.com*
Alex Roszkowski. Account Manager… *ar@monocle.com*
Sanne Visser. Senior Project Manager – Creative Solutions
Guido de Boer. Publishing Executive – Asia… *gb@monocle.com*
Patrick Owens. Advertising Executive… *po@monocle.com*
Clare Burger. Advertising Operations Assistant… *cb@monocle.com*

ADVERTISING OFFICES
Hans Otto. Zürich (SWITZERLAND)… *hans.otto@i-plus.ch*
JoJo Wang. Hong Kong (HONG KONG & CHINA)… *jw@monocle.com*
Nartnittha Jirarayapong. Bangkok (THAILAND)… *noo@njintermedia.com*
Keith Lee. Taipei (TAIWAN)… *leekh@ms4.hinet.net*
Atsushi Saito. Tokyo (JAPAN & KOREA)… *ast@monocle.com*

CIRCULATION & SUBSCRIPTIONS
Holly Anderson. Head of Circulation & Brand Partnerships… *han@monocle.com*
Birute Kaluzeviciute. Circulation & Subscriptions Marketing Executive… *bk@monocle.com*

BUSINESS DEVELOPMENT
Martin Vigren. Market Director (ITALY)… *mv@monocle.com*
Cindy Chan. Commercial Executive (ASIA PACIFIC)… *cch@monocle.com*

RETAIL
Zeid Habayeb. Acting Head of Retail… *zh@monocle.com*
Simone Werger. Product Development Manager… *sw@monocle.com*
Marie Absire. E-commerce Manager… *ma@monocle.com*
Effie Vasil. Merchandising & Supply-Chain Manager… *ev@monocle.com*
Shaun Barneveld. Logistics Executive… *sb@monocle.com*

CUSTOMER SERVICE
Lina Constanza Mendez Saenz. Customer Service & CRM Manager… *lcms@monocle.com*
Charlotte Sachs Customer Relations & CRM Coordinator… *cas@monocle.com*
Benson Batty. Customer Relations Assistant… *bb@monocle.com*

FINANCE
Jörg Meiner. Chief Operating Officer… *jm@monocle.com*
Pauline Ho. Group Treasurer… *pho@monocle.com*
Kirk Manhin. Finance Manager… *km@monocle.com*
Philippa Cooper. Finance & Business Development Manager… *pc@monocle.com*
Luigi Zanfino. Head of Accounting… *lz@monocle.com*
Doria Kolli. Credit Controller… *dkk@monocle.com*
Achira Ramjanally. Accounts Payable Coordinator… *ary@monocle.com*
Danica Fernandes. Accounts Assistant… *df@monocle.com*
Saiwa Afzal. Accounts Receivable Assistant… *sa@monocle.com*
Rahina Mumuni. Cashbook Accountant… *rmu@monocle.com*

THE BOARD
Richard Atkinson, Tyler Brûlé. Directors
Tyler Brûlé. Chairman

HEAD OFFICE
Midori House
1 Dorset Street, W1U 4EG
TEL: +44 (0)20 7725 4388
info@monocle.com

EDITOR IN CHIEF'S SUPPORT
Hannah Grundy.
Communications & Project Manager… *hg@monocle.com*

FRONT OF HOUSE
Lauren Doughty.
ld@monocle.com

BUREAUX
Toronto
776 College Street, ON M6G 1C6
TEL: +1 647 694 2626

Tokyo
1F, Luna Rossa
1-19-2 Tomigaya
Shibuya-ku, 151-0063
TEL: +81 (0)3 6407 0350

Hong Kong
1–4 St Francis Yard, Wan Chai
TEL: +852 2804 2323

Zürich
90 Dufourstrasse
CH-8008, Zürich
TEL: +41 44 368 7000

Los Angeles
Platform, Unit 105
8820 Washington Boulevard,
Culver City, 90232
TEL: +1 310 982 2966

SHOPS
London
2A George Street, W1U 3QS
TEL: +44 (0)20 7486 8770
londonshop@monocle.com
Zeid Habayeb: *zh@monocle.com*

Hong Kong
Shop 1, Bo Fung Mansion,
1–4 St Francis Yard, Wan Chai
TEL: +852 2804 2626
hkshop@monocle.com
Harry CK Wong: *hw@monocle.com*

Peninsula Hotel, Salisbury Road,
Tsim Sha Tsui
TEL: +852 2812 7886
peninsulashop@monocle.com
Harry CK Wong:
hw@monocle.com

Toronto
776 College Street, ON M6G 1C6
Tel: +1 647 694 2626
torontoshop@monocle.com
Zeid Habayeb: *zh@monocle.com*

Tokyo
1F, Luna Rossa, 1-19-2 Tomigaya
Shibuya-ku, 151-0063
TEL: +81 (0)3 6407 0845
tokyoshop@monocle.com
Junichi Toyofuku: *jt@monocle.com*

Merano
23 Via Dante, 39012
meranoshopshop@monocle.com
Linda Egger: *ge@monocle.com*

Zürich
90 Dufourstrasse, CH-8008
TEL: +41 44 368 7001
zurichshop@monocle.com
Raffael Lienert: *rl@monocle.com*

Los Angeles
Platform, Space 105, 8820
Washington Boulevard, Culver City
TEL: +1 310 982 2966
lashop@monocle.com
Sam Jones: *swj@monocle.com*

Milan
Tenoha Milano,18 Via Vigevano,
20144
TEL: +39 02 8088 9147
milanshop@monocle.com
Benedetta Pozzi: *bp@monocle.com*

TRAVEL RETAIL
Hong Kong
Hong Kong International Airport,
Gate 61, Terminal 1
TEL: +852 2116 5530
Cindy Chan: *cch@monocle.com*

MONOCLE CAFÉS
London
18 Chiltern Street, W1U 7QA
TEL: +44 (0)20 7135 2040
Zürich
90 Dufourstrasse, CH-8008
TEL: +41 44 368 7001

KIOSKAFÉ
London
31 Norfolk Place
London W2 1QH
TEL: +44 (0)20 3111 4242

The MONOCLE
FORECAST

Dream. Shop. Experience.®

PHOTOGRAPHERS. WRITERS. ILLUSTRATORS.

The political, economic and cultural events of 2019 have been tumultuous but we've unearthed the people and stories that suggest there's plenty to be positive about in 2020. And who better to send out into the big wide world – to find out what's going on, where it's happening and why – than our talented contributors? Let's meet some of them.

Though she loves to cook, writer **Wendell Steavenson (1)** is also partial to visiting *French bouillons (page 164)*, the informal mess halls of Paris that are enjoying something of a revival. She finds it difficult not to order bone marrow on toast when she sees it on the menu but one of her favourite things about these bustling restaurants is that it is easy to order two or three small plates – to compose a light lunch of your own – even when your companion is tucking into *steak frites*.

But he really had to wrap up warm for a trip to remote Mongolia, where he documented the ways in which catch-and-release fly-fishing have helped to save taimen, the world's largest trout, from extinction. His hardiness came in handy for his trip to the foothills of the Rocky Mountains for THE FORECAST. There he turned his focus to *Boulder (page 51)* in the US state of Colorado for our Small Cities Index.

Lyndee Prickitt (4) knows a fair bit about life in India: the native Texan, who was born in Alaska, has set up home in New Delhi with her Indian husband, their daughter and "a lot of air pollution". Her reporting career has included interviewing Benazir Bhutto on a plane full of her rowdy supporters as she left Dubai to return to Pakistan; her dispatch on *The Times of India (page 44)* was just as lively

Karina Tsui (2) wrote her thesis at New York University on the history of political performance art in Hong Kong, where she is currently based. It was good preparation for her recent exploits: reporting on the ongoing – and violent – pro-democracy protests in the city. For THE FORECAST she took a break from dodging tear gas and rubber bullets to travel to Seoul, where she *talked to a K-pop agent (page 89)*. And she might well be whistling some well-known Korean tunes in her free time, which she most likes to spend hiking to beaches to swim in the sea.

Photographer **Kyle Johnson (3)** is no stranger to the cold and his connection to the wilderness around his native Seattle informs the style and composition of his work.

an assignment. When she's off duty she can often be found strolling through New Delhi's picturesque Jodi Gardens or experimenting with Indian ingredients in cocktails. Cheers!

Illustrator **Massimiliano Aurelio (5)** grew up in Taranto, a picturesque coastal city in Puglia in southeast Italy. But rather than kick his heels on the sole of Italy's boot, he moved to Milan in 2003 via Rome, where he studied visual arts at the Istituto Europeo di Design. His keen eye and steady grip came in handy when it came to sketching the artwork for *30 ideas for 2020 (page 107)*, our rundown of ways to make it a good year. Massimiliano's tips? Enjoy the city you live in, make time to read and prioritise the company of your loved ones. Sound advice. — (M)

ILLUSTRATOR: MAYA STEPIEN

The MONOCLE FORECAST

Poliform

RIDING THE WAVES

Cleaning up Krakow, preserving the skills of Portuguese artisans and naming the president of Switzerland: the year ahead is set to be full of challenges. We meet the people who are finding solutions to the issues on their doorstep, from Helsinki to Ho Chi Minh City.

The new Maine attraction
Lobster country turns to kelp

The lobster roll from Red's Eats lobster shack, which overlooks Sheepscot River in Wiscasset, is arguably the best in Maine. Customers queue for hours for a pile of fresh, hot lobster meat atop a hotdog bun. Maine has seen record harvests in recent years; statewide catches were worth more than $484m in 2018. But the changing climate could mean that the crustacean won't always be so readily available. Lobsters make up three quarters of the state's fishing income but they don't like warm water – and 2019 was the hottest year on record.

Entrepreneurs believe that kelp is at hand. The seaweed grows in shallow coastal waters and might yet ensure the financial success of fishing in Maine. Abigail Carroll returned from Paris in 2009 to launch Nonesuch Oysters in the Scarborough estuary. Its skincare products made from kelp help to balance the books off-season. Lisa Scali, Tollef Olson and Mitch Lench's company, Ocean's Balance, sells seaweed-based products such as kelp purée and wakame flakes. "Seaweed was interesting to me from an ecological, sociological and business perspective," says Lench. "Seaweed is the most nutrient-dense plant on the

earth and it captures carbon. Seaweed goes beyond food: it provides solutions."

Briana Warner (*pictured*) agrees. Her firm, Atlantic Sea Farms, helps Maine's fishermen to diversify their income. "We provide seeds, help them get leases, provide training and buy everything they grow," she says. The firm then turns the seaweed into food products to sell to natural-food stores in the US.

The potential global market for edible seaweed is expected to hit $8.8bn (€7.9bn). Too good to be true? Scientist Nichole Price, from Maine's Bigelow Laboratory for Ocean Sciences, is optimistic but watchful. "Maine has the capacity to support seaweed aquaculture that is therapeutic to water quality," she says. "But we need to grow the industry in a sustainable way." — AMG

Foundation class
Architecture school for children

Seven-year-old Oscar is building an overpass with wooden blocks and glue. He places a bucket of playdough on top to test its sturdiness. "It needs to be high enough for boat traffic to pass under it and strong enough to withstand cars and pedestrians," he says. The bridge holds the weight but fails a more important test: Oscar's friend Miio smashing it to pieces. The boys burst out laughing.

The Arkki School of Architecture in Helsinki is no ordinary architecture school. Children aged four to nine are learning the basics of building – and having fun while they're at it. "We give them problems to solve, tasks that are rooted in their own world," says teacher (and architect) Minna-Mari Paija. "We don't lecture and we don't use books."

In one class the pupils are building miniature deep-sea exploration vessels; in another they are designing transformable houses. The shelves are brimming with their earlier creations: it's a wonderful glimpse into the boundless imagination of small children. "Why can't we build houses underwater?" says nine-year-old Sofia. "It would be so much more fun to look at fish instead of walls." She is surrounded by models

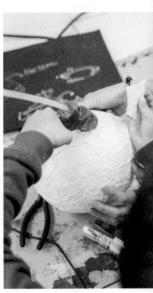

> **"Why can't we build houses underwater? It would be so much more fun to look at fish instead of walls"**

of everything from hillside housing to imaginary cities, skyscrapers and castles.

Founded in 1993, the school now attracts about 800 pupils a year for its extracurricular courses – and that's just in Helsinki. Arkki School also has outposts in China, Thailand, Vietnam, the Czech Republic and Greece. With urbanisation around the globe showing no signs of slowing down – and likewise concern about climate change – the role of sustainable architecture is only going to gain importance. Educating the next generation of architects – or, simply, anyone who lives in a city – from a young age is a smart thing to do, particularly as the children here seem to be taking to the task with an enthusiasm unmatched by adults.

More often than not the architectural training that these children receive goes beyond the classroom. Some parents say that they've woken up in the middle of the night to find their offspring engaged in urban planning. Not all of them will end up pursuing what they've learnt at Arkki as a career but school director Jaana Räsänen is no less satisfied. "Some of our pupils have become architects but that's not our goal," she says. "We want to raise citizens who understand the importance of architecture in creating a good living environment for us all." — PB

Smog burner
Krakow tackles air pollution

Pawel Scigalski, Krakow's minister for air quality, is pointing to a map on his computer showing the city's pollution levels; the centre is a resassuring green. But when his finger moves across the map to Krakow's outskirts, where the map turns red, his smile fades. While the situation is improving, the city and its surroundings still often accumulate pollution.

Krakow's air is some of the dirtiest in Europe so the city has had to take a proactive approach to solving its problem. The situation is improving but 33 of the 50 most polluted cities in the EU are in Poland. Why? Coal is still the main source of domestic fuel; politicians here have dubbed it "black gold".

Krakow's turnaround is the result of activists and campaigners fighting for the city to clean up its act. For the past five years the municipality has been phasing out solid-fuel boilers and stoves; a complete ban on burning coal and wood came into effect this September. The tipping point, though, was a petition and mass protest organised by Polish Smog

Alert. The campaign group now runs workshops to explain the dangers of breathing polluted air. "It's not like air pollution wasn't around before Polish Smog Alert started in 2013," says the group's Magdalena Kozlowska. "But people didn't say anything so politicians didn't need to do anything about it."

The conversation has also spurred entrepreneurs into action. Start-up Airly provides detailed pollution readings via its smart sensors, a service it sells to local governments. It was founded by friends who were training for a marathon but couldn't get readings that would help them decide where to run. "The younger generation in Krakow is amazing," says Airly's Marcin Gnat. "They have the guts and talent to change things." There are now more than 200 sensors in the city and some 250,000 people accessed Airly's online map last year.

Activists and the government will be keeping a keen eye on smog levels here. Both believe that regulations have to be implemented across the entire country but the links between those in power and the mining industry are still too entrenched. Change is the air though. "What's happening in Krakow proves that it is possible," says Gnat. — SZ

No place to hide
Cock an ear to lipreading

It's morning in a London café and the co-working crowd have settled in. I'm trying to guess what people are saying but I can't make out the words over the din. But Tina Lannin can follow every word. Lannin is deaf but she can lipread from six metres away. It's key to her ability to understand people and her primary means of making a living: she is the founder of forensic lipreading firm 121 Captions.

It seems that I'm not the only one who's curious to know what people out of earshot are talking about: the media's desire to find out what public figures are up to off-mic has created a high demand for lipreaders. Lannin's first projects consisted of trying to work out what people were saying in the background of

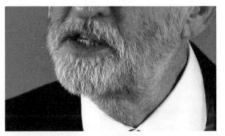

extremist ransom videos. "It was harrowing," she says. "The work bookings slowly build up; the celebrities and politicians came later."

Nearly half her work is for newspapers and TV stations seeking to break stories on indiscreet outtakes; a 20-second video can take hours to decode. She was asked to lipread comments made by UK opposition leader Jeremy Corbyn (*pictured*) in 2018; he was accused of calling Theresa May a "stupid woman" but claimed that he had said "people". "The shape of the words 'people' and 'woman' are completely different," says Lannin.

Accuracy is of the utmost importance. That's why Lannin employs seven lipreaders – at least two working on each project to verify results. All of the staff are deaf; Lannin says that it's a pre-requisite for a good lipreader: "If you've been lipreading people all your life you should be good at it." — NM

PHOTOGRAPHERS: JUHO KUVA. ILLUSTRATOR: DIRK SCHMIDT. IMAGES: SHUTTERSTOCK, GETTY IMAGES

Picture postcards
Something to write home about

Daniel Ulrichs works with global artists to produce covetable artworks in the form of a €1.50 postcard. "The first print run was 10,000 with six or seven artists; I thought they would last five years," he says. "In six months we were sold out."

That was in 2015. Now the business – based in Galway, Ireland – produces 40,000 cards a year. Ulrichs has worked with 40 artists, printing some 700 works as postcards, greetings cards and posters. Last year he launched publishing firm Artwerk Press, which commissions 12 in-house artists to create exclusive pieces. Most recently he started selling his postcards wholesale; 12 retailers in Ireland and abroad have stocked up. For all the fears that postcards might soon become a vestige of the past, Ulrichs' business sends a hopeful message.

Creating a publishing company in Galway wasn't easy. Ulrichs was running his family toy shop, The Wooden Heart, when he decided to pursue something that resonated more deeply with him. "I loved design, architecture and art," he says. He realised that he had to establish the market he wanted to sell to. "I had to create something that would bring people through my doors. That's where we looked at coffee."

Coffeewerk + Press became known for the quality of its roast and the deft hands of its baristas. Ulrichs knew that this would draw attention to the other wares in his shop. It's easy to walk out with more than a cup of coffee. Customers flick through cards divided by artist, from surreal mushroom illustrations by Amy Ross to monochrome collages by Larissa Haily Aguado. The first floor is filled with design objects; Futagami's brass trivets sit beside earthenware from Arran St East in Dublin. The second floor is a poster gallery.

By the window, two residents are enjoying a coffee. Ulrichs' international vision is kept alive by the community. "It's great that young people find us," he says. "But the 60-year-old couple who come in every Sunday – that's what warms my heart."— LHO

"The first print run was 10,000 with six or seven artists; I thought they would last five years. In six months we were sold out"

Mind your business
Mass-scale meditation

My eyes are closed and the room is silent but for the droning of a *shruti* box: an Indian instrument that's similar to a harmonium. The 320-strong audience has been asked to repeat a humming sound; my voice wobbles before latching on to the correct pitch. I'm at The Big Quiet, a mass meditation series launched in New York in 2015. Four years later the company embarked upon a US roadtrip, visiting 10 cities. This event, at the 1895 McKim Building at Boston Public Library, is the last stop.

Founder Jesse Israel starts with an icebreaker. Members of the audience are asked for their name, go-to karaoke song and a description of something they've done for themselves recently. Then come the breathing exercises, which include raising our hands and pulling them down with a shout and making animal noises. Next up are a series of mindfulness exercises before the 75-minute event is wrapped up with musical performances.

Even though I was expecting a little more quiet time than I ended up getting, there's no doubt that Israel and his team are on to something. Everyone seems to want a piece of the wellness pie, whether it's luxury hotel brands or start-ups working on mobile apps – and it's a trend that looks set to continue in 2020. But the more meditation gains ground, the more it is being sold. Does something so personal remain effective on an industrial scale – and with such high production values?

PHOTOGRAPHERS: CODY O'LOUGHLIN, LOI XUAN LY

Israel says that the motivation to found The Big Quiet came from his own experiences of feeling anxious and lonely in a big city, and the realisation that "the thing we crave most is human connection". But the 35-year-old realises that not everyone engages with the New Age, incense-burning idea of spirituality. Instead his aim has been "to create entry points that make these experiences more accessible", which is why he sees the nexus of music, entertainment and brand collaborations playing a part in The Big Quiet's future. He hopes to take the firm's events overseas and deliver mass meditations to as many as 20,000 people at a time.

While I didn't quite achieve spiritual enlightenment on this soggy evening in Boston, I realise that the path is a long one. Yet I'm a little disappointed with myself: while we were being asked to concentrate on our heartbeat, I found my mind wandering. Israel says that this is perfectly normal – but I'm reluctant to confess that it landed on what I was having for dinner. — EJS

Everyone seems to want a piece of the wellness pie, whether it's luxury hotel brands or start-ups working on mobile apps

From Shanghai to Saigon
French expats ditch China for Vietnam

Maison Marou, a Parisian-style café-cum-chocolate factory in Ho Chi Minh City, is abuzz with customers. Founders Samuel Maruta and Vincent Mourou (*pictured*) are in expansion mode: a third outlet is due to open in 2020. The city's booming F&B industry is attracting fresh talent. "Saigon [as residents still call it] feels like Shanghai did at the start of the decade," says Maison Marou's Julie de Bruyne. For many the change has been more noticeable over the past few years. when cars became commonplace and modern homes started to dot the skyline. "Saigon is a magnet for young French," says Maruta.

Ho Chi Minh City is opening its doors at the same time that Shanghai is shutting up shop. French entrepreneurs are nudged towards the door while aspiring graduates, who are struggling to get visas, are heading to Vietnam instead. "In the government's eyes, every foreigner working in China is stealing the job of a Chinese person," says De Bruyne, who often bumps into friends from Shanghai in Ho Chi Minh City.

"Saigon feels like Shanghai did at the start of the decade"

China's policy shift is heavy-handed but it is also a sign of Shanghai's progress: regulations are up, corruption is down and outside talent is surplus to requirements. Henri-Charles Claude, country manager of building-management firm Aden Services (one of the largest French-owned employers in Vietnam), moved to Vietnam in 2015. "Foreigners still had a value in Shanghai back then," he says. "We would never move back to China now."

Internet censorship, pollution and China's social-credit system, which ranks citizens on their contribution to society, are particularly galling for French expats. But the sun is shining in Ho Chi Minh City and its growing French population is intent on making hay – and plenty of chocolate. — JCH

Lean times
New York's 'pencil towers'

Winds of 88km/h aren't ideal for riding to the top of what is soon-to-be the world's slimmest skyscraper, although it might be a good moment to see if the "tuned mass damper" – an anti-wobble device – is working. But the hoist running up the side of the building will only take me as far as the 43rd floor today – about half way up. A few days later I finally have the chance to stand on the roof, 388 metres above Manhattan. It's a clear day and the views of George Washington Bridge to the north and One World Trade Center to the south are impeccable. Fancy a penthouse? It's a snip at $50m (€44.5m).

The building in question – 111 West 57th Street – is set to welcome residents in spring 2020. It is part of a mutation of New York's skyline. Just over a decade ago only two of the city's buildings – the Chrysler Building and the Empire State Building – were "super-tall"(more than 300 metres high). Now there are almost 30. "Pencil towers" are all the rage. These slimline buildings are the result of expensive land, and an insatiable appetite for luxury and technical breakthroughs, such as the ability to produce concrete that's two-and-a-half times stronger than previously achievable for shear walls.

These slimline buildings are the result of expensive land, and an insatiable appetite for luxury and technical breakthroughs

There's no doubting the architectural merit of 111 West 57th Street, which has a width-to-height ratio of 1:24. "We wanted to look at the history of the tower in New York and extract the DNA of the buildings that the city loves," says Gregg Pasquarelli *(pictured, on right)*, a founding principal at Shop Architects, the firm behind the design.

The tower wraps around an existing building from 1925: the former Steinway showroom. Its landmarked interior rotunda will become a retail space. But it's the new façade that stands out. More than 41,000 pieces of terracotta and bronze filigree line the east-west shear walls; the north-south faces are wall-to-ceiling glass overlooking Central Park. "The best view of the best view in New York," says Michael Stern *(pictured, on left)*, CEO of developer JDS. But not everyone is as excited: pencil towers are a symbol of the 1 per cent. Stern thinks there's a disconnect between perception and reality: he says that the shadow projected by slim buildings passes quicker than that of larger towers.

The trend for super-tall buildings raises important questions. Architect Felipe Correa of Brooklyn's Somatic Collaborative asks, "How does the city see the larger social landscaping changing?" Let's hope that it won't skimp on size and ambition there either. — EJS

Preserving the past is Portugal's best route to the future

Look, it's Mr Whatsisname
Who is Switzerland's president?

Name the first 10 foreign national leaders who come to mind. It is likely that most will be buffoons or monsters; such are the creatures that get most of the press. So if an inept or malevolent leader is a surefire guarantee of notoriety, is the inverse true? Is it the case that well-run countries do not have well-known heads of government? Another challenge: name the president of Switzerland, by any measure one of the world's best-run countries. If you can't, don't beat yourself up. On a recent assignment to Geneva, I asked a dozen or so people that very question; barely a handful knew the correct answer.

"I'm sure most Swiss people don't know who the president is," says professor Pascal Sciarini of the University of Geneva. "But the word has a different meaning in Switzerland." This is true: Switzerland's presidency is a

Heart of craft
How Portugal is preserving its artisans' skills

Inside a workshop in Lisbon's Ricardo do Espírito Santo Silva Foundation, French designer Sam Baron is watching Portuguese craftsmen work on moulds for a mirror's decorative reliefs. The piece, which will be adorned with plated leaves, is part of his latest collection. The designer is calling it "Feuillade", a play on the French word for "leaves" and the Portuguese *saudade* (longing). The object is a meeting point not just for Portugal and France but also past and future.

Many designers appreciate the value of traditional crafts but it is not always easy to find artisans who are willing to experiment. That's where Passa ao Futuro (Pass to the Future) comes in. The nonprofit organisation arranges collaborations between Portuguese artisans and international designers. "It's about attracting young blood and understanding that these people carry important knowledge," says Fatima Durkee, who founded the firm with her partner Astrid Suzano in 2016.

The pair realised that a lot of artisans were about to retire, taking their skills with them; the solution was to involve young creatives and direct artisans towards new ventures. Passa ao Futuro isn't the only group to have understood that preserving the past is Portugal's best route to the future.

A sticker reading "Lojas com História" (Shops with History) graces more than 140 storefronts in Lisbon – a city hall initiative that protects commerce which has long shaped the city's economic, cultural and urban landscape. There's a candlemaker that's been active since 1789, a tea and coffee dealer that opened in the 1940s and Versailles Tearoom (*pictured*), which was founded in 1922. Álbio Nascimento is one of the curators of the project and says, "We are trying to create a network so that people notice that there is a historical social fabric." — GSL

collective role. The top tier of the country's government is the seven-member Federal Council, elected by the Swiss parliament. Every year a member of the Federal Council is named president of the Swiss Confederation. In 2019 it was Ueli Maurer of the Swiss People's party; in 2020 it is due to be the current vice-president Simonetta Sommaruga of the Social Democratic party. It is unclear how many of her fellow citizens will be aware of this. "A lot depends on how much a president tries to be visible," says Sciarini. "Sometimes they get to the end of their year and nobody has really noticed them."

So can this model can be exported? "I wouldn't claim that the Swiss system can't be exported," adds Sciarini. "But it is part of a much larger set-up that is quite specific to Switzerland: the system of federalism, direct democracy and popular initiatives."

Which could be where the fantasy of quietly competent leadership founders: we might have to do more of the work ourselves. — AM

PHOTOGRAPHERS: RICKY RHODES, RODRIGO CARDOSO. ILLUSTRATOR: DIRK SCHMIDT

ESCAPE PLAN

James Chambers REPORTING FROM
Indonesia: The country will soon have a
new capital if the president's ambitious
(some say unlikely) plan comes to fruition.
While there's an argument for leaving
Jakarta, would a new seat of government
be an improvement?
PHOTOGRAPHER *Muhammad Fadli*

Indonesia's Ministry of National
Development Planning enjoys a pleasant
view of Jakarta. Bappenas, as the ministry
is known, looks out over Suropati Park, a
picturesque square with sculptures and a
fountain in the low-rise residential neighbourhood of Menteng. The latter is an
example of Dutch urban-planning in what
was then colonial Batavia. When the sun
shines, residents sit on the benches and
stroll along the pavements. Embassies on
all sides add to Menteng's similarity to
London's gilded Mayfair.

However, the ambassadors and minis-
terial staff may soon be looking for a new
home. Indonesia has decided to move its
national capital and Bappenas has been put
in charge of planning the yet unnamed new
seat of government. Relocating to the rainforest island of Borneo is arguably one of
the most ambitious urban-planning endeav-
ours of this kind ever undertaken – by any
country – and 2020 will be a make-or-break
year for the mega project.

President Jodo "Jokowi" Widodo wants
to spread economic opportunity away
from the island of Java, where the majority of Indonesians live, and take some of
the burden off of the former 17th-century
Dutch trading hub. "The new capital could
be another source of growth and we want
Jakarta to heal a little bit," says cabinet minister Bambang Brodjonegoro, who headed
Bappenas from 2016 to 2019. Construction
is slated to begin by the end of 2020 and
the first Indonesian government workers
should be moving there in 2024 (although
the whole project will take decades).

"Our president wants to be different
from other presidents: he wants to realise

1

his vision," says Bambang, who was in charge of picking the site of the new city. Jokowi called him to the presidential palace in 2017 and instructed him to find a suitable site in Kalimantan, the southern part of Borneo controlled by Indonesia. He had been working on the project for two years before the president went public with the move in August 2019. "It has to happen by the beginning of 2024 because the president's term will end in October 2024."

This ambitious – some might say unbelievable – timetable also reflects the sense of urgency around the notion of leaving. Menteng's pavements, planned gardens and greenery embody everything that Jakarta is not. The Indonesian capital is a chaotic and sprawling city of some 30 million people crowded into *kampungs* (urban villages), with little public space or public transport. Streets often flood during the rainy season due to poorly maintained pumps and drainage canals that are clogged with rubbish. About 40 per cent of Jakarta is below sea level. Some districts are said to be sinking and the city sits on an earthquake zone.

Even on a good day the cluttered streets are filled with a cacophony of cars, bikes and food carts. For officials, getting around without a police escort can be arduous. Jakartans tell stories of taking 2.5 hours to travel 5km.

Jakarta's problems are nothing new; nor is the plan to move the capital. Jakartans have heard it all before. Sukarno, Indonesia's post-independence leader, floated the idea of shifting to Borneo in the 1960s. An alternative plan by one of his successors to move to nearby Jonggol was scuppered when rampant property speculation pushed up the cost of land. So scepticism is understandably rife, although Jokowi would have voters believe that this time will be different. For one thing the government already owns the land: 40,000 hectares of rainforest that has been earmarked to house some 1.5 million people.

Previous spread:
1.
A light-rail transit being built in Jakata's Kuningan area

This spread:
1.
Pedestrians in central Jakarta
1.
Traffic jams are a familiar sight in the city

"The big question on many people's lips is why now?"

Many countries have moved capitals before or are in the process of doing so (*see panel, next spread*); what sets Indonesia apart is the scale of its ambition. The likes of Australia, South Korea and Malaysia selected sites that were in striking distance of the largest city. Conversely, Kalimantan is on an entirely different island – a two-hour flight away from Jakarta. Bambang draws comparisons with Brazil. The Latin American giant moved its capital from Rio de Janeiro to the more central Brasília; the capital today has a population of about 3.5 million.

"Brazil did it in five years back in the 1950s," says Bambang confidently. And it's true that technology advancements should work in Indonesia's favour – plus, the government isn't starting from scratch because the selected coastal site is near two existing cities. Therefore contractors can make use of existing roads and an airport, as well as a sea port; that's advantageous when shipping in construction equipment.

The need to address imbalances is another similarity. While Brazil's economic powerhouses are clustered on its east coast, Indonesia's are concentrated on the western island of Java. Jokowi wants the government to jumpstart economic activity in the eastern archipelago and start narrowing the income disparity between Java and the other islands. According to Bambang, "The disparity between western Indonesia and eastern Indonesia has been stagnant for almost 40 years."

Both countries also picked a symbolic location in the geographic centre of the country. This is especially important in Indonesia, a sprawling archipelago made up of more than 17,000 islands and multiple languages, cultures and religions. East Timor gained full independence in 2002; recent riots in Papua have reignited the spectre of eastern separatism.

Nevertheless, the big question on many people's lips, especially in the business community, is why now? A tight government budget, combined with a plan to partly fund the project with private money, would be severely tested by any major shocks to an already slowing global economy.

At the same time, residents of Jakarta are beginning to see some improvements in their city thanks to infrastructure investments, which began when Jokowi was governor and sped up under his successor Basuki Purnama. Upgraded flood defences, new toll roads, an Uber-like ride hailing service and the city's first subway have all made life easier for Jakartans – and some are determined to stay. Regional association Asean has a brand new HQ and secretary-general Lim Jock Hoi has announced that the secretariat will remain in Jakarta, comparing it to the UN in New York. Jakarta, like New York, will continue to be Indonesia's primary economic hub.

1

Unsurprisingly the word "legacy" quickly comes up in conversation. "He wants to have this as part of his legacy," says Bambang, who can attest to Jokowi's personal interest in the project. "The longest discussions I've ever had with the president during his first term were whenever we talked about the new capital."

A €30bn price tag has been put on the relocation plan. While this figure is almost certain to rise, the political costs of securing Jokowi's legacy could be even higher. "The project needs buy-in from parliament and the public, not just the president," says Phillips Vermonte, director of the Centre for Strategic and International Studies, a Jakarta-based think-tank. That includes securing legislative support beyond Jokowi's administration.

Jokowi's success in winning re-election for a second and final term masks a complicated web of political horse-trading. His majority in parliament relies on a fractious coalition of parties and the country's growing religious conservatism is forcing the liberal president into uncomfortable and uncharacteristic compromises. Controversial laws rushed through by the

2

1.
Scavenging at a temporary rubbish dump in Pluit, north Jakarta

"Concerns about building a city amid ancient rainforest will take more assuaging"

1

Past pastures new:
Indonesia has plenty of historical precedents to learn from; here are a few examples.

Canberra
The most boring city in Australia can still inspire

Canberra has long carried the mantle of being Australia's dullest metropolis but there's nothing dull about the city's origins. Chicago architect Walter Burley Griffin, who is nowadays hailed for his visionary approach to the city's plans, won an international competition and moved to Canberra in 1914, leaving behind a thriving practice in Chicago, a city that boasted revolutionary architects such as Frank Lloyd Wright.

Griffin's plans were inspired by the site's natural surroundings. "He really wanted to build a Washington DC, a city that people would find inspiring, and for it to be a great nation-building moment," says Christopher Vernon, an associate professor at the University of Western Australia's School of Design. But when he arrived he found that budgets were tight and suspicion of (non-British) foreigners was high. Facing stiff resistance, he quit the project in 1920 after being edged out of his leadership role; a new committee opted for suburban sprawl rather than the high-density city Griffin had planned.

Canberra became a budget version of Griffin's grand vision and what started out as a compromise capital, midway between Sydney and Melbourne, is only now starting to find its own identity. Griffin's original design did inspire other cities – including New Delhi and Rio de Janeiro – so perhaps Indonesia's capital can draw some inspiration too. — AB

Islamabad
Capitals can move – and so can their political problems

Islamabad's planned grid of wide streets is a car driver's dream when compared to the commuting chaos of Karachi but the new capital is by no means insulated from the country's political jams: the airport is a regular target for domestic terrorist groups and hotels are mini-fortresses. Indonesia faces its own security challenges: religious conservatism is on the rise and terror attacks often threaten Jakarta. A new capital will need security to be built into the foundations; this will require architects and urban-planners to be particularly smart. Residents want a liveable city, not a police state. — JCH

Nur-Sultan (Astana), Kazakhstan
Beware too much symbolism

Moving the capital from Almaty to Astana was billed as a nation-building exercise by the country's first post-Soviet president, Nursultan Nazarbayev. However, after two decades of authoritarian rule and dozens of architectural monstrosities, it has become a living monument to the man himself. The "leader of the nation" stepped down in March 2019 and Astana was promptly renamed Nur-Sultan in tribute.

Indonesia's brief for its masterplanning competition calls for a sustainable and adaptable forest city, so it would do well to stick to the script. Fortunately it doesn't have Kazakhstan's oil money to squander. — JCH

outgoing parliament caused student riots and several deaths. There is some suggestion that he let lawmakers pass a bill to rein in Indonesia's powerful anti-corruption agency to win support for his capital project.

Likewise the public still need to be convinced. A nationwide poll conducted by Median after the decision was announced in August suggests that support for the project hangs in the balance, though approval numbers are likely to go up as more concrete plans emerge (scant details have been revealed so far). Government plans to invest in Jakarta would also assuage fears that the current capital will be unceremoniously abandoned and left to sink into the sea. "There is no really strong rejection of this plan," says Daliana Suryawinata, co-founder of architecture firm Shau. "People get that we need to develop something and Jakarta will not lose from not being the capital."

However, environmental concerns about building a new city amid ancient rainforest will take a lot more assuaging. According to Bambang, the land is already being used for commercial gain and many of the adjacent forests have already been stripped by illegal loggers. But political promises to build a sustainable and adaptable forest city that fits in with the natural environment inspire little confidence in a country dogged by corruption and a poor environmental record.

The upcoming year will be decisive; even if, as most suspect, building contractors do not manage to break ground by the end of 2020. The next major milestone will be coming up with a palpable masterplan. "Year one is most critical to the success of a 30-year masterplan – can you get people to buy into it and feel like it's theirs?" says Sylvester Wong, head of Asia Cities at architecture firm Aecom. "Unlike architecture, masterplanning is very ego-less. You have to be willing to let everyone feel that it's theirs."

1

2

Wong is working on New Clark City, which is being built by the Philippine government north of Metro Manila. He recommends that the Indonesian government plans for 100 years and then breaks it into five-year segments, so that there are bite-sized chunks for private investors to get involved in. "A good masterplan is a nimble framework that allows the unpredictable to happen," he says.

While Jokowi has been criticised for a lack of public engagement over the new capital, he appears to be listening. An early government masterplan was scrapped in favour of a competition open to both domestic and international entrants; the in-house design, when viewed from above, was meant to resemble the mythical Garuda bird that appears on Indonesia's state emblem, resplendent with a feather, wreaths and a Washington-style obelisk at its centre.

A promising judging panel has been appointed and the winner will receive a relatively sizeable design fee. Such a set-up is a rarity in Indonesia and recognises the long life of the eventual design. Daliana Suryawinata will serve as one of the 13 jury members alongside Ridwan Kamil, who is the architect-turned-politician who transformed Bandung as mayor before becoming governor of West Java. "As a country it would be our first time planning a new city so it excites me as an urban designer – it gives me hope," says Suryawinata.

Her excitement is shared by notable Indonesian architects and there is a consensus forming about the need for efficiency: saving space, saving resources and reducing commuting times. A small capital, both in terms of its population and architecture, needn't be seen as a sign of failure – nor lack of ambition. In this way, Indonesia can break away from comparisons to Brazil's capital. "Brasília was designed during a time when the only way to show identity was through monumentality," says Suryawinata. "Is that still the case? I hope not." — (M)

Q&A
Milton Braga
Architect

Milton Braga, an award-winning architect and professor who's the author of an influential book about the pilot plan for Brasília, says the Brazilian capital (inaugurated in 1960) began as an architectural highlight – but forgot to plan for urban sprawl. — LE

How did Brazilian authorities decide who would design Brasília?
There was a competition to present a masterplan for Brasília. Oscar Niemeyer was contracted by Lucio Costa, a student of the famous modernist architect Le Corbusier, to fulfill his winning pilot, assessed by an international jury. It was an extremely intellectual period in our history and the architects were prepared.

Is it considered the true capital of Brazil?
Cities are not a physical product – they're a process. You can build a bunch of houses with almost utopian levels of over-planning but it is what comes after the architecture that matters. Culturally Brasília has become a big urban centre, with a thriving popular-music scene and a first generation that strongly identifies with being from the capital. The social question for the most part has worked and it has achieved the main objective of moving the focus of our country away from the coast.

What is the biggest challenge for Brasília now?
Brasília suffers from the same problems as other major cities when they start to populate. The original plan was designed for roughly 500,000 residents – fast forward 60 years and more than 3.5 million people live in Brasília and its outskirts. The horizon stretches away endlessly so the suburbs have sprawled with no proper development plan in mind, which has led to issues with infrastructure and housing. On top of that you add the broader issues in Brazil: poverty and inequality.

What can other cities learn from Brasília?
There was a big technical debate at the time about how to develop the city: engineers said Brasília needed a proper network of satellite towns, roads and flight paths built around it if the project was ever going to be a success. Fifty years ago many of the northern states in Brazil simply didn't exist, so planners failed to imagine how the pilot might expand. We thought it was just one big building project, not a transformative process. That is worth considering when building something that will last for centuries.

What's it called? The tricky game of naming a new city

Delving into history, while tempting, can dig up old memories. The US chose to name its capital after the first president and one of its greatest statesmen when it built Washington in 1790. Indonesia is likely to land upon its own founding father: Sukarno. As president he proposed the idea of moving the capital to Kalimantan (albeit a different area). "Sukarno City" would also win political support from Sukarno's daughter, Megawati, an ex-president who wields considerable power. However, the leader of Indonesian independence went on to rule with an autocratic iron fist. A new name would offer a cleaner slate. — JCH

IN IT TOGETHER

Michael Booth REPORTING FROM *Denmark:* In these digital times, loneliness – where it comes from and how to solve it – is a key issue for countries. Danes, the world's most enthusiastic participants in clubs and societies, may have the answer. PHOTOGRAPHERS *Jan Søndergaard & Kristian Holm*

The Scandinavians are a famously collectivist bunch but the Danes' social cohesion is off the scale. The superglue that binds them is an extraordinarily high membership of clubs, societies, voluntary associations and unions. According to one recent survey by Aalborg University, more than 90 per cent of Danes are members of something or other. The Danes joke that if two or more of them meet they will form a *forening* (a union or association) and they commonly refer to their country as *foreningsdanmark*.

Some say this tendency has something to do with climate or geography; others point to Denmark's history, in which its vast empire was slowly eroded by military defeats and economic ruin, leading to an insular national character. These nesting tendencies are inherent in hygge, the much co-opted Danish concept of cosiness.

"Denmark is a small country; we don't really have any natural resources so we've had to work together to negotiate and trade," says social scientist Torben Bechmann Jensen from the University of Copenhagen. The upside might well be that this proclivity to join groups and clubs is the secret behind Denmark's most valuable soft-power asset: happiness.

Club membership has also helped make Danes among the least lonely people in the world. In a 2018 Eurobarometer survey, 79 per cent of Danes reported never or almost never being lonely and only 8 per cent of them socialised less than once a month. In contrast, more than one in five American and British adults reported feeling socially isolated; while two in five people in Japan are expected to live on their own by 2050.

"After a dip in the cold water we're smiling, even at the end of a bad day," says

1.
Members of Charlottenlund Søbad winter-bathing club prepare for another bracing dip
2.
These brave women are among the 3,900 Danes signed up to the society

The average Dane belongs to three clubs, more than any other European nationality

Karen Sophie Lerhard, a board member of Charlottenlund Søbad winter-bathing club. "We dream of the ice; the colder the better." Fellow board member Lise Bak agrees: "The slush is like a silk scarf on your body."

Winter bathing is just one of the club activities booming in Denmark. Charlottenlund Søbad, founded in the early 1900s on the coast just north of Copenhagen, has 3,900 members and a 14-year waiting list. The health benefits of a cold dip are well documented but the winter bathers stress the social aspect. "You feel part of something bigger here," says new member Lotte Maersk. "It becomes part of your identity: 'I am a winter bather.'"

There are said to be more than 100,000 local and national societies and associations in Denmark, ranging from hobby or leisure-orientated groups with a handful of members to trade unions, which have a combined membership of about 1.25 million. The average Dane belongs to three such formal associations, more than any other European nationality. The most popular are amateur football clubs, with 350,000 members nationally.

In recognition of sports and hobby clubs' importance to Danish society, support for them is enshrined in law and local authorities provide financial assistance and help in finding premises. But Bechmann Jensen does have a warning about *foreningsdanmark*, pointing out that if you're constantly told that you live in the happiest country in the world but you yourself aren't happy, it can foster a sense of failure and isolation. "Younger Danes and those in big cities are occupied with other things and the fear of missing out stops them committing to something regular," he says.

**Do you socialise less
than once a month?**
(2018 EU survey)
Least lonely three:
Denmark: **8** per cent said yes
Netherlands: **8** per cent
Sweden: **8** per cent
Most lonely three:
Greece: **40** per cent said yes
Hungary: **40** per cent
Lithuania: **35** per cent

1

2

1

2

Psychologists have long cited membership of groups as important for wellbeing. A 2016 Nottingham Trent University study of 4,000 people in Italy and the UK found that for each club, team or group people joined, their happiness increased by 9 per cent, irrespective of age, gender, income, employment status or nationality.

"In a sense it doesn't matter so much what people do in the club – it doesn't have to have a greater purpose," says Bechmann Jensen. "The most important thing is just to be doing something with other people."

around a board game," he says. "You don't have to talk too much. Everyone has been really welcoming."

A couple of days later we catch up with another Danish special-interest club: the Realdania By og Byg Klub (Realdania City and Construction Club). Realdania owns about 60 historical buildings across the country, including several homes created by Danish design legends such as Arne Jacobsen and Poul Henningsen. Today some of the club's 4,000 members are in Brabrand, west of Aarhus, visiting a prime

3   4

The members of Københavns Braetspilsklub (Copenhagen's Board Games Club) would probably agree. At a weekly Tuesday night gathering in a basement in an apartment block in Nørrebro, members cheerfully suggest that board games are a rather limited sphere of activity – but that's the point.

"It's great to be with people while you are doing something else, something distracting," says Daniel Olsen as he enjoys Great Western Trail, an obscure and complex strategy game typical of those played here. "My friends and family are all members of clubs but I was a bit socially distant. Then I found board games and it was like, 'Where have you been all my life?'"

Another student, Copenhagen-based Louis Kleiminger, a first-time visitor, reveals that he sometimes finds social occasions stressful. "It's easy to be with people

1.
Realdania By og Byg Klub members, correctly shod
2.
Knud Friis' house, Aarhus
3.
The dice roll again at the Board Games Club
4.
Plenty of options for the Copenhagen players

example of 1950s Danish brutalism that was once home to its architect, Knud Friis.

"This is different to other clubs I belong to," says Pia Mølholm, who's also in a salsa club and a business networking association. "This is about an interest in architecture, not so much about hygge or getting together to eat and drink." Similarly, another member visiting the Friis house, Maike Jessen, belongs to a knitting circle and a ceramics club "but this is about an interest in design. I don't come here [just to] socialise."

Whether it's about socialising or not, the simple motivation for joining a club is the same: get out of your home, follow your passion and be less lonely while doing it. "You work to get results and be productive," says Stine Petersen, another member of multiple organisations. "But these clubs are where you put your love." — (M)

SAFILO

MADE IN ITALY DAL 1934

THOUGHT LEADERS

We explore the 2020 agenda for three globally focused think-tanks, from tackling alternative facts in the US through consensus and compromise to pushing the bigger picture in India – plus the future of Europe.

Rand Corporation

Location:	*Santa Monica*
Founded:	1945
Staff:	1,950

These days Michael D Rich is preoccupied with "truth decay". The term, coined by the Rand Corporation, describes what the think-tank sees as the diminishing role that facts and analysis play in public life. It's a familiar issue today with "fake news" and "alternative facts" but Rich, Rand's president and CEO, says the danger has been brewing for decades – and will take decades to undo. Rand has researched the topic in the US and next year plans to look at Europe. "Facts are facts," says Rich. "People can interpret a situation differently but a resolution is not going to be possible if we can't agree on the facts."

In an imposing building a pebble's skim from Santa Monica Beach, Rand has come a long way from its roots as a scientific research institution. It conducts some of the US's most important research on global policy in areas such as education, ageing societies, healthcare, migration and gun reform.

Rand was initially a private offshoot of Douglas Aircraft Company, a top defence contractor, and provided analysis and data for the US airforce – but by 1948 it had evolved into an independent non-profit. In the mid-1950s it started to diversify, first with other national security clients, then adding social and economic policies. One of its most significant developments came in 1970 when it founded the Frederick S Pardee Rand Graduate School, one of the eight original public policy schools in the US and the first to offer a PhD on the subject. "It was crucial for Rand to become both a research and educational organisation," says Rich.

It now spans nine locations, with dozens of academic disciplines under its belt, and has expanded from its national focus to an international outlook. "What hasn't changed is our non-profit charter," says Rich. "And our core values: quality and objectivity." — CCR

1

World view
Michael D Rich

What is the biggest threat for 2020?
Truth decay. One point that we've made over and over again is that no important problem can be solved in the US within the span of just a four-year presidency or a two-year Congress. And the way those problems have been surmounted in the past is consensus and compromise. That's impossible if two sides can't agree on the basic facts.

Which other key issues are a focus in the year ahead?
We are going to issue major reports on the opioid crisis that's affecting the US.

And we'll continue to expand our work on the effectiveness of different gun policies.

And outside the US?
Some countries face challenging demographic trends, particularly refugees and internally displaced persons. The challenge is to provide adequate education and healthcare for the families that have been displaced, as well as assisting countries in integrating them into their economies.

Who will have the biggest global impact in the next year?
Whoever is the winner of the 2020 presidential election in the US. I'm not in a position to predict – none of us are. But whoever prevails in that contest will have a tremendous impact on the world.

Institute of Defence Studies and Analyses

Location: *New Delhi*
Founded: 1965
Staff: 110 (50 admin, 60 research fellows)

India's Institute of Defence Studies and Analyses (IDSA) sits on one of the world's most critical geopolitical faultlines. As nuclear-tipped allies Pakistan and China look over India's shoulder, the IDSA advises the government on everything from border security to nuclear armament. But its scope goes far beyond the country's backyard.

The IDSA was founded in 1965, modelled on the US's Rand Corporation, and now collaborates with dozens of think-tanks around the world. Its flagship publications, the *Journal of Defence Studies* and *Strategic Analysis*, cover a broad range of issues, from the Syria-Turkey conflict to xenophobia in South Africa. Though it is autonomous, it is entirely funded by India's Ministry of Defence.

Ambassador Sujan R Chinoy took over as director-general earlier in 2019. A career diplomat, Chinoy has focused on helping Indian officials, from soldiers to students, see the bigger picture. An officer on the Pakistani border might know about cross-border terrorism but little about wider relations with China, or how his decisions might impact India's economic growth, so the IDSA offers courses that it hopes will make soldiers better decision-makers. It also runs programmes with young parliamentarians who may sit on important committees in the future, and even engineers in the arms industry. "I want them to know more about what their equipment ends up doing, in whose hands, and why it gets used," says Chinoy.

He adds that as nationalist sentiments soar, Indians have become preoccupied with defence, making the IDSA's outreach more pressing. "It's not with ecclesiastical zeal that we try to convince people to come around to our point of view. The point is to familiarise people with broader issues." — LLP

IDSA's 2020 priorities: Terrorism and radicalisation; stable relations with China, Pakistan and the Indo-Pacific region; upgrading India's domestic defence industry; climate change's impact on regional and energy security; fallout from a fractured, multi-polar world.

Previous page:
1. Rand
CEO Michael
D Rich

This page:
1.
The IDSA's
Sujan R
Chinoy
2.
Clingendael's
stately home

"We want to help a Dutch audience make sense of what's happening abroad"

Clingendael Institute of International Relations

Location: *The Hague*
Founded: 1983
Staff: 100 (11 different nationalities)

Approaching Clingendael on an autumn day is a feast for the senses. Bowing trees along a narrow road envelope you under falling leaves; only the occasional sheep disturbs the silence. Bags of ripe apples and pears from surrounding orchards sit in reception – a gift from the farm sharing this forested land on the northeastern outskirts of The Hague.

The stately 17th-century manor, which now houses the institute, was the residence of the occupying Nazi commissioner in the Second World War. Tank barriers and pillboxes are also a diverting attraction for visiting diplomats and dignitaries. "It works as a very good ice-breaker," Rem Korteweg, a senior research fellow, says of the site's history.

Clingendael was founded in 1983, in a merger of five smaller Dutch institutes and think-tanks. In its early years the institute was closely aligned to the Dutch government but today, while it still receives more than half of its funding from the Dutch government, it is politically independent and has become a leading global voice on international affairs. "On the one hand we make sense of the Netherlands to an external audience," says Korteweg. "But we also want to help a Dutch audience make sense of what's happening abroad."

Clingendael has 100 staff producing extensive research on international issues and hosting an ambitious events programme. The manor and grounds are also home to the Clingendael Academy, which trains diplomats, NGO staff and civil servants from the Netherlands and all over the world. Students can also take courses in diplomacy, conflict-resolution and mediation, all informed by a uniquely Dutch foreign-policy outlook shaped by centuries of trade and empire. Korteweg describes this perspective as a "pragmatic and open approach to international affairs". — CMG

Clingendael's 2020 priorities: Europe's future after Angela Merkel; Brexit and uncertain effects for the Netherlands; the Sahel region and curtailing people smuggling; an end game for Syria's civil war; elections in the US and Taiwan.

PHOTOGRAPHERS: ANKUSH MARIA, JUSSI PUIKONNEN

1

BAIA

THE BIG NEWS

Lyndee Prickitt REPORTING FROM *New Delhi:* Covering everything from entertainment and spirituality to politics and crime across a staggering 56 daily editions, the 'Times of India' is the most widely circulated English language newspaper in the world. Read all about it.
PHOTOGRAPHERS *Ankush Maria & Saumya Khandelwal*

It's 06.00 and Ram Lakhan jostles for position among the other delivery men as bundles of newspapers are dropped from the backs of the *Times of India*'s trucks onto a road in New Delhi. He now has less than two hours to race through the narrow streets and up and down the apartment-block stairwells of his patch, a middle-class neighbourhood, to ensure that his customers get their paper in time to read with their morning tea. He's one of 30,000 deliverymen across the country who are a vital part of the machinery that has helped the *Times of India* (TOI) retain its title as the most widely circulated English language newspaper in the world.

An hour later, another group of the newspaper's early birds – crime reporters based in more than 50 Indian cities – begin their morning calls to police stations, finding out what went down in

the dark of night. One of New Delhi's three crime reporters is Somreet Bhattacharya and this morning – as every morning – he has spent an hour talking to groggy night-shift officers before he heads out to follow up on leads and catch up with investigators in person.

"It's not always easy waking up to news of suicides and murders, being on the phone all day, but it's the job," says Bhattacharya, who has been at the paper for seven years and has broken stories about a national kidney-extraction racket and the murder of a politician's son.

Back in the newsroom he sits down to start filing the five to

"We've deepened our coverage with more news, more data, more graphics"

seven stories that he's expected to deliver every day. This is also the point in the morning when the political and law reporters, gearing up to stalk the halls of government and court houses, are heading off on their daily hunt for news.

But it's not just politics and crime that will fill the 30-plus pages of the *Times of India* today. There's a city reporter writing a story revealing that New Delhi's electric rickshaws, meant to decrease pollution levels, are actually running on cheap, dirty fuel. Another reporter is assessing whether a massive hike in traffic fines is taming India's notoriously unruly roads.

Unlike many of the country's politics-heavy newspapers, the TOI has a more popular approach to news, offering stories that it hopes will appeal to India's growing middle class. Much like India itself, the paper is crowded and colourful, with headlines in different fonts, bright sidebars, photos everywhere and lots of huge adverts. Very lively.

It's a far cry from the staid, colonial paper it once was. Originally called the *Bombay*

1.
New Delhi printing press – Asia's biggest – on the outskirts of the city
2.
Story discussions
3.
On newsstand
4.
Layout checks

Times, it was founded in 1838 to inform the British ruling class and business elite. But as India has changed, so has the TOI, often called the "masthead of India". After the British left in 1947, the paper championed the nation's early development and socialist values. But when the markets began to liberalise in the 1990s and a more consumerist middle class emerged – people with interests beyond activism and politics – it gained a different audience. Its cultural reference points no longer looked westward but were proudly rooted in homegrown entertainment, food and fashion.

The owners of the paper today are two business-savvy brothers, the third generation of their family to be at the helm of a company still known formally by its old English title: Bennett, Coleman & Co. They have capitalised on India's changing demographics and turned the firm into a media empire. The younger and more public of the brothers, Vineet Jain, is a 53-year-old whose quirky specs and boyish smile belie the sharp-shooting businessman beneath.

"The paper used to be really thin: 12 pages," says Jain. "Now it's three to four times that, including supplements, as we've dramatically deepened our coverage with more news, more data, graphics and perspective." Jain is managing director of the firm,

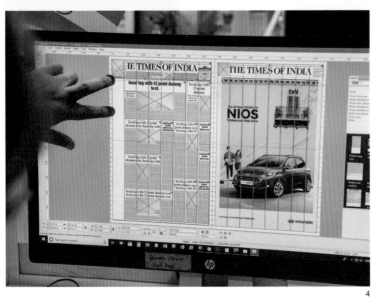

which also owns 13 other publications, 12 TV stations, 76 radio stations and a fledgling university.

Sitting on the ninth floor of one of the company's many buildings, he smiles proudly as he likens the TOI to the original tasting plate of Indian dishes. "The paper is like a thali, a buffet of India. We offer the entire spectrum, from politics and crime to fashion, sports and spirituality."

But being in step with its readers (the paper puts its daily print circulation at 4.2 million, which continues to grow) is not simple in a country with a vast mix of cultures, languages, religions and, at times, contradictions. The paper puts out a staggering 56 editions every day, with five to seven pages of "hyper-local" news in each one.

This mammoth task of publishing so many editions is not just about giving readers a bespoke product but also driven by the lure of tapping regional businesses, which would not be able to afford ad space in a national paper. "India's smaller tier-two cities are expanding and new wealth is being created," says Jain. "Literacy is also rising. We want to cater to this audience."

By the afternoon the senior editorial team begins its day, arriving at the paper's main newsroom in New Delhi, near the seat of government, in a utilitarian building owned by *The Indian Express*. This drab base is temporary: a fire destroyed TOI's editorial headquarters in 2017 and a new building is being erected.

Three people gather around the desk of Shankar Raghuraman, a softly spoken senior editor who

India's print-digital news diet:

News consumers in India have long bucked the global trend in their preference for old-fashioned ink on paper. But as 610 million Indians now have smartphones, (a number expected to nearly double by 2024) there is a steady move from print to digital. According to TOI front-page editor Vikas Singh, research shows that readers use digital throughout the day, while the newspaper is reserved for breakfast and leisure time. That's when readers can linger over analysis pieces, editorials and features, usually while sipping some masala tea. "That's the 'tea' in the TOI," says Singh, smiling.

TOI is the largest English-language newspaper in India but there are local language papers with higher numbers. See right for the top five, based on circulation in the second half of 2018.

India's top sellers:

4.32
MILLION
Dainik Bhaskar
Language: *Hindi*

3.41
MILLION
Dainik Jagran
Language: *Hindi*

3.03
MILLION
Times of India
Language: *English*
(4.2 million if including discounted distributions)

2.37
MILLION
Malayala Manorama
Language: *Malayalam*

2.07
MILLION
Amar Ujala
Language: *Hindi*

1

2   3

1.
Delhi city reporter Paras Singh investigating rumors that electric rickshaws are running on dirty fuel
2.
Shankar Raghuraman, senior editor with Times Insight Group
3.
Checking proofs
4.
Printing press in action

4

flap": a vertical half page that sits on top of the front page. This week the team is looking at the data on school lunches, digging into everything from nutritional value to how much money is set aside to pay for them. They have found that many states don't issue enough funds to cover the cost of a healthy lunch.

The political editor Rajeev Deshpande says that besides covering the horse-trading of India's coalition government, he must also surrender column inches to other concerns, such as education and gay rights. "The paper tries to catch these moments, moving away from a world in which we're just looking at parliament and policy."

At 18.30, 19 senior editors enter the long conference room that's flanked by large video screens showing the group's news and business TV channels. Printouts of dozens of stories from different departments and regions are looked over while everyone waits for editor in chief Jaideep Bose to dial in to the meeting from the TOI's original HQ in Mumbai. Much like Charlie in the 1970s TV show *Charlie's Angels*, Bose is just a voice, avuncular but commanding, and everyone leans in when he offers his opinion as to the worthiness of a story.

During the meeting, the front-page editor uses pen and paper to draw and redraw the front page, which can have as many as eight columns of text carrying up to 20 stories, covering everything from the situation in Kashmir to the state of coral reefs. Bose does not lead the meeting but shepherds it with the grace and authority of someone respected. When we later visit the Mumbai newsroom he declines to be quoted, preferring, he says, for his work to speak for him and his editors to take the limelight.

runs a small and earnest team of data-crunchers. Their attention flits from various spreadsheets they've mined from government, corporate and NGO databanks as they work on uncovering stories buried in the data.

Take, for example, the paper's recent "lost votes" stories. The team exposed India's anachronism of only letting people vote from the place they are registered in, without any postal vote as an alternative. After running the numbers for the previous national election, the team found that an astonishing 280 million people – a third of the electorate – were not able to cast a vote in the ballot. For weeks leading up to May's general election, the paper ran profiles of "lost voters" and graphics decoding the numbers.

This statistical storytelling is so popular with readers that it regularly features on the inside of the paper's innovative "front

1.
Main New Delhi
newsroom
2.
Ready for the
delivery boys to
make their mad
dash across India

Unlike many of the Indian newspapers losing readers to digital platforms that deliver content to smartphone users, the TOI has seen an upsurge in its print circulation. Executive editor Diwakar Asthana puts it down to the paper's centrist and populist approach. "We get attacked by everyone, whether it's the opposition or the government, BJP or Congress – whether it's left-wing or right-wing. That shows we're doing something right. We don't pontificate as much as other Indian papers. We're not preachy. We believe we don't have to torment our reader every morning."

Asthana points to a more frivolous recent story about a young man who pushed his BMW into a river out of anger after his father refused to buy him a Jaguar. "More cerebral papers wouldn't want to waste space on such a story."

Such is the premium that the paper places on lifestyle and entertainment news that it publishes a daily 12-page supplement on such topics – and that can double in the festive season. It also offers "hyper local" content with 46 city editions. Its newsroom is across town in Delhi's "film city" and its editor, Anshul Chaturvedi, reports directly to managing director Jain. "We handle all the stories that happen in people's supplementary time," says Chaturvedi. "Everything they do when they clock off from

"We don't pontificate as much as other Indian papers. We're not preachy. We believe we don't have to torment our reader every morning"

work is what we report on. And our casual tone and language reflect that."

The supplement's special Delhi correspondent, Divya Kaushik, has spent the day writing a consumer guide to spotting sketchy massage parlours. However, by the evening she is reporting on a fashion show that's featuring young designers, with a special appearance from Miss India.

Back in newsrooms across the country, after a strictly vegetarian buffet is served, only the sound of concentration (and the occasional order barked across computers) can be heard as the midnight publishing deadline looms. The last of the seniors to leave is front-page editor Vikas Singh. "I try to unwind but I stay awake next to my phone for another two hours. Just in case."

Then it's over to the dozens of printing presses up and down the country. While they run all day to produce the group's other publications, they now whirr only for the flagship TOI, heralding another day in India. — (M)

Delhi office
Meet the editors

Shankar Raghuraman
Senior editor, Times Insight Group

A former business journalist, now in charge of the TOI's data-mining team, dissecting everything from politics to cricket with fastidious glee.

Neelam Raaj
Editor, Sunday Times

Makes sure the news gets more depth and analysis in the weekend papers. Married to a journalist at another paper – she's glad hers is number one.

Vikas Singh
Front-page editor

The last editor to leave the building and doesn't get to bed till after 02.00. When he's not catching up on sleep he writes novels in his spare time.

Subhendu Mukherjee
City editor for Delhi

A harmonica player who enjoys being outraged at how politicians promise much but deliver little. Loves Delhi, even though his family is from Bengal.

Rajeev Deshpande
Political editor

Covers India's dance with democracy. Having grown up when there were just two kinds of chocolate bars in India, he enjoys charting the nation's growth.

Diwakar Asthana
Executive editor

Says the TOI succeeds because it's not elitist. Likes it when it pushes social norms, whether women's rights, gay issues or fighting for better nightlife.

Bavaria is Great for Business.
No Brexit. No Uncertainties.

With Brexit imminent and its ramifications far from clear, the only certainty for businesses in Britain is uncertainty. Companies, founders and innovators are concerned about continued access to the EU market, the UK's leading trading partner by far, attracting overseas talent and tapping international research networks. So why not have a look at Bavaria, a safe haven to mitigate such concerns. Explore one of Europe's top ICT, technology and manufacturing hubs. Our service is confidential and free of charge.

→ www.invest-in-bavaria.com/brexit

SMALL PACKAGES

Looking to escape the metropolis to downsize? Our global network of correspondents have come up with a definitive list of the world's best small cities, which provide the right balance between opportunities for rich cultural experiences on your doorstep and that all-important space to breathe.

A new decade, a new city? How about fleeing that busy metropolis and downsizing? Is it possible to have it all – the job, social life, family, a well-connected airport – away from the capital in a cosier place? We believe it is – and we're backing the 2020s as the decade of the small city. So we've selected the world's best for your consideration.

"But wait – why should I want to move to a small city? I'm happy here!" We hear your rebuttal from the sophisticated suburbs of New York, Hong Kong and Sydney. Small cities aren't for everyone but the best ones can offer life-enhancing qualities. For one, your finances go further – whether you're homemaking or setting-up shop.

Small-city living isn't just about space and comfort – although the idea of a vegetable garden to call one's own has its appeal. And socially, life can feel refreshingly different in a more community-minded place. Big cities bring people closer together but often only in a practical sense: isolation and loneliness seem to be unavoidable by-products. The best small cities tend to provide the opposite: people are more relaxed and happy to have a chat. While your social calendar may start off looking sparse upon arrival in a good small city, it doesn't take long to become integrated.

Urban dwellers have also become a more health-conscious bunch and small-city living can aid your mental and physical wellbeing. Beyond a better connection to the outdoors, the reduction in pollution, lack of traffic and additional breathing room result in a healthy antidote to the hustle and bustle of modern life.

The places we have chosen (and see page 55 for how we chose them) are also good for doing business in, while technology is freeing up how and where we work. Still unsure? Tour through our Small Cities Index and see what's on offer; you might be surprised to learn that downsizing your city can increase your quality of life. — (M)

❶

Lausanne, *Switzerland*

Between Geneva and Zürich, perched on the north bank of Lake Geneva, Switzerland's fourth-largest city is worth stopping in – or, indeed, staying in. Small enough to feel familiar, big enough to live in, this city of 140,000 inhabitants has something to offer at every stage of life: good schools, top universities, professional opportunities (combined with ease of travel) and a slower pace of life in later years.

Stone buildings, with shutters in soft green, chalky blue and dove grey, give Lausanne an elegant, almost-Mediterranean vibe. On its charming streets, shops sell goods ranging from flaky croissants to antiquarian books. It is built on a slope, rising more than 500 metres from the lakeside port of Ouchy to Chalet-à-Gobet, where the celebrated École Hôtelière is located. This makes cycling tricky but it's more than made up for by the metro – and it's the smallest city in the world to have one. Sustainability reigns too, from investing in renewable energy sources to 350 hectares of parks and gardens.

Despite Lausannois' relaxed manner, their city has a reputation for international excellence that belies its size. The École Polytechnique Fédérale, specialising in science and engineering, has numerous spin-offs, and the École Hôtelière tops global hotel-management school rankings. The city is also hugely international: more than 40 per cent of its population is foreign. And since 1994 it has proudly held the title of Olympic Capital, as the base of the International Olympic Committee. Further along the lake, the Olympic Museum and Olympic Studies Centre make Lausanne the global centre for knowledge of the Games.

If Lausanne's streets start to feel too narrow, the lake and mountains are within easy reach. Geneva Airport is a 45-minute train ride away and there are direct rail connections to Milan and Paris (both under four hours). Yet with this small city's pleasures – a glass of local wine, a shimmering view of the lake – always within arm's reach, there is not much reason to leave. — ABC

Best for: Diversity. Lausanne is an international city, despite its size, and you'll hear French, German and Italian spoken, plus English in accents from Australian to Canadian.

What's needed: Lausanne is Switzerland's third-most expensive city to rent an apartment in. More affordable housing is needed, especially for families. The third metro line, set to open in 2026, will further improve public transport.

Life after midnight? Yes. Start the evening with wine before moving to one of the city's clubs or music venues.

Small cities – the rules:

A city of 200,000 people provides something of a sweet spot when it comes to offering an optimum balance of social and cultural diversity and quaintness. Our list comprises places as close to this mark in population as possible (some are smaller, some a tad bigger). To determine a shortlist our global correspondents scoured their home regions, weeding out cities lacking close connection to an international airport, decent public transport, progressive local government and welcoming residents.

After drawing up a shortlist we delved into the harder metrics such as crime rates, life expectancy and quality of universities. We then contrasted them with more intangible factors, such as whether you can get a good coffee at 06.00 or be on a dance floor at 02.00. Finally we dispatched our journalists to spend some time in our list-toppers to meet the locals and ask an important question: why is your small city one of the world's best?

❷
Boulder, *USA*

It's worth rising early in Boulder to drive the short distance to the start of the Chautauqua trail. As the sun comes up you can take in vistas of the city and the breathtaking Flatirons: jagged rockfaces that dominate the scenery. If any proof were needed of the quality of life in this city of 108,000, nestled in a valley near the Rockies, it's here. With sunshine about 300 days a year, Boulderites are an outdoor tribe.

Boulder was popular with the Beat generation: its Trident bookshop and café, originally the Buddhist Bookstore, dates back to 1979; Allen Ginsberg was a faculty member of the Buddhist-inspired Naropa University. The 1960s and 1970s were key decades, when the "elders" (as those still alive today are called) established environmental rules such as a maximum building elevation of 16.8 metres – the rough height of a cottonwood tree. It was around then that Boulderites voted to tax themselves to fund land acquisition (something everyone is very proud of): the city owns and manages more than 18,000 hectares of parkland. Meanwhile the neat centre boasts restaurants, such as Corrida and Frasca, that wouldn't look out of place in major metropolises (not to mention the rare cheese and meat at Cured).

Almost all native and adoptive Boulderites say the sense of community and talent pool were decisive factors in staying. Boulder is home to 17 federally funded labs, a large University of Colorado campus, renowned advertising firm Crispin Porter Bogusky and design and consultancy firm Stantec Vibe. There's something fascinating about the currents moving through this place, from tech start-ups to regenerative farming projects via health-food brands. Boulder punches above its weight because it seems to have perfected the work-life balance (people "work to live" here, according to one Boulderite).

Think you'd still miss the big smoke? Probably not. But if you did, Denver – with its international airport – is but a 45-minute drive away. — EJS

Best for: Media. Boulder is served by Denver television and radio stations, newspapers and other media. There are a number of outlets but the newspaper of record is the *Daily Camera.* NPR affiliates include Colorado Public Radio KUNC and Boulder has a community radio station, KGNU.

What's needed: The city needs to solve how to grow to suit all parties, be it outwards or upwards. Transport links have to be improved to make it easier for people to commute into the city and avoid congestion on the road.

A good coffee at 06.00? One of many examples is Ozo Coffee, which started in Boulder and has several locations.

3

Bergen, *Norway*

Folks from here will argue that even the capital Oslo can't offer the *friluftsliv* (outdoor life) Bergen provides. The city is surrounded by picturesque mountains and is a gateway to the fjords of Norway's western coast. Recreation options, besides hiking, include summer dives into seawater pools, winter train journeys and ski resorts in Voss and Geilo. The wet weather can be tiresome but it has proven useful in creating a buzzy hospitality and dining scene that's enlivening the city's once-tame nightlife. Let's hope retailers will follow suit, as current shopping options are lacking. Bergen's creative industries, however, are thriving, nurtured by talent from well-respected universities and growing amid handsome studio spaces, often housed in remarkably revived industrial buildings. — ZZ

Best for: Culture lovers. Bergenfest is a world-leading summer music festival, while Kode and the recently renovated Natural History Museum don't disappoint on the cultural venue front.

What it needs: A good coffee shop for early birds.

Cycle-friendly? Yes. Bikes are a popular means of commuting and the city is cycle-friendly.

PHOTOGRAPHER: THOMAS EKSTROM

Hobart, *Australia*

This petite city is often bathed in moody sunlight, boasts a mild climate and has a resident mob of wallabies. Views include the peak of Mount Wellington, modernist suburbia and salty seafarers hauling the latest catch into port. But don't let this laidback feel fool you: Tasmania is the second-best performing state economy in Australia. Though this has been stimulated by a migrating workforce. Hobart remains one of Australia's most-affordable state capitals. There's an exciting thrum here too, yet the test will be how local and state governments capture the momentum. It has been suggested that the city needs a further 20,000 people to bolster the economy; move here and start living the good life. — MKA

Best for: Education. The University of Tasmania is a leader in marine and Antarctic science.
What it needs: Critical investment in streetscapes, its transport infrastructure and the housing mix.
Cycle-friendly? Mayor Anna Reynolds wants more bike lanes but car remains king for some voters.

Chigasaki, *Japan*

Surrounded by mountains and ocean, and just an hour's train ride south of Tokyo, Chigasaki feels like a rural refuge. Good cycling infrastructure means two wheels are the the best way to get around and to visit beach communities nearby. International cuisine options aren't limited to the centre as the whole city is dotted with good restaurants. With its mild climate and safe streets, this is a quiet Tokyo alternative. — AAF

Spots to surf, hike or ski? Chigasaki is famous for surfing. The Shonan coast is the birthplace of Japan's modern surf culture.
Best for: Young families. The council has introduced initiatives for working mothers and it's a very safe city.
What it needs: Lacks good offices and co-working spaces at reasonable prices. The Chigalab co-working space is a nice try but there's room for improvement.

Bolzano, *Italy*

Widely considered one of Italy's most liveable cities, the capital of South Tyrol has plenty on offer for nature lovers and entrepreneurs alike. It is in the heart of the Alto Adige region, dotted with top-class resorts where ski slopes stretch for miles. Recently a steady growth in the number of start-ups has seen a focus on tech innovation, supported by the autonomous region's wealthy economy and a generous grant scheme. What's more, Bolzano can pride itself on reliable transport and an extensive network of cycle lanes. — GDE

What it needs: The city has a small airport but no scheduled passenger flights. Ideas to open it up to airlines have been met with fears of mass tourism.
Best for: Wine-lovers. Alto Adige white wine is among the best in Italy – and that's saying something.
Good local media? Newspapers are *Alto Adige* and *Dolomiten*; radio stations include RAI (local edition).

Bordeaux, *France*

Despite its neoclassical architecture and surrounding wine region, Bordeaux has been more generally known for traffic jams and abandoned warehouses. But thanks to a significant effort to revitalise the Garonne River it has become France's relaxed alternative to Paris. A buzzing technology scene and renowned restaurants are attracting young professionals escaping the capital's exorbitant living costs. The inauguration of Méca, a new cultural hub designed by Bjarke Ingels Group, aims to broaden access to the arts. Getting around is pleasurable too: it's one of the most bicycle-friendly cities in the world. — JWE

Best for: Cyclists. Besides the city, they can enjoy the vineyard-laden routes.
What it needs: A mayor to fill the large shoes of the outgoing one: former prime minister Alain Juppé.
Life after midnight? Bars at the Quay de Paludate are busy into the early hours.

Innsbruck, *Austria*

Set amid the fine scenery of the Alps, Innsbruck is Austria's mountaineering capital but it offers much more than skiing and hikes. It's built majestically, from its alley-woven old town with its handsome 19th-century Tyrolean State Theatre to the contemporary masterworks from Zaha Hadid and Snøhetta that dot its slopes; the wealthy city's coffers have gone a long way to beautifying the place. Good weeknights out occur regularly, with its university crowd fuelling a vibrant bar and restaurant scene that sizzles on long summer nights. And cabin fever is rarely a feature of life here: Munich and Bolzano are both less than two hours away by car and Zürich is a little further down the road. — ZS

Best for: Skiers, snowboarders or anyone with a passion for the slopes.
What it needs: A few more international residents beyond the friendly locals who call it home.
A good daily paper? *Tiroler Tageszeitung* does a fine job of covering the province and is proudly published in Innsbruck.

Porto, *Portugal*

Porto's transformation from a sleepy city into a spritely alternative to Lisbon continues at full speed. Fifteen years ago this was a city in decline as Portugal's economy faltered but a shift in priorities – restoring the historic cobbled and tiled centre, spending on infrastructure and opening up to foreign investment – has propelled Porto forward. It's a creative melting pot, with proximity to good fashion and furniture manufacturers drawing a smart crowd of designers. The sunshine and world-leading cuisine are encouraging foreigners to settle here. — CCR

Best for: Beach lovers who don't mind the nippy Atlantic temperature.
What it needs: More money spent upgrading its historic core; many buildings sit derelict.
Well connected? Besides its international airport there's a train connection to Vigo, which joins Spain's high-speed rail system.

Aachen, *Germany*

This German spa town hugs the border of the Netherlands and Belgium, making it a cultural melting pot despite its size. It's well connected via road, rail and now air, thanks to the renovated Maastricht Aachen Airport. Besides historic landmarks, crowned by the Unesco World Heritage-listed cathedral, it boasts a number of museums, plus four colleges and universities. It is a youthful city and there's a growing start-up scene. Housing remains affordable enough, though prices are rising quickly. Free time can be spent in the nearby forests, fields and thermal springs – or tackling the region's best beer at one of the city's many pubs. — MSS

Best for: Start-ups. Well connected and loaded with talented students, it's a fine launching point for business.
What it needs: More affordable housing for its young talent.
Good daily paper? The award-winning *Aachener Zeitung*.

Reykjavik, *Iceland*

Home to little more than 100,000 people, Reykjavik's rare traffic jams keep the air clean and commutes short. Despite its isolation, international tech firms based here take advantage of the easy direct flights from both Europe and the US. And a decade on from the country's economic meltdown, start-ups are flourishing. Business aside, the city is dotted with geothermal swimming pools and is a short drive away from geysers and waterfalls. The world's northernmost music festival, Iceland Airwaves, attracts thousands of foreigners every November, when tourism begins to slow. The quieter months are no bad thing for locals as limited housing stock and high seasonal demand has led to steep living costs and fewer long-term rental properties. — GDE

Best for: Architects. The city requires new buildings – and fast.
What it needs: Smarter governance on leveraging tourism.
Life after midnight? Bars and clubs stay open late at the weekend.

Savannah, *USA*

With its tree-lined streets and rich architectural heritage, Savannah feels like nowhere else in the US: wander around the extensive historic district and you'll come across styles spanning Italianate, Gothic and more. Founded in 1733, it is steeped in history yet the city is forward looking. The food scene has plenty of contemporary offerings (try Squirrel's in the Starland District) and the art scene is buzzing, anchored by the Savannah School of Arts and Design, one of the country's (if not the world's) best arts institutions – it also has an excellent museum. And then there's the easy access to nature, surf and sandy beaches: Tybee Island is about 20 minutes from downtown. What more could you ask for? — EJS

Best for: A slice of old America.
What it needs: Better housing and addressing its wealth inequality.
Connections: Savannah/Hilton Head International Airport handles more than 40 non-stop flights per day.

Potsdam, *Germany*

A relaxed urban retreat a mere 40-minute drive from the capital, Potsdam is a better option than a Berlin suburb for those curbing their night-time activities as they grow a family. The peaceful streets here, adorned with 18th-century palaces and lush parks, provide the perfect antidote to the nightlife-driven German capital. The city's lakes make it especially desirable in the summer, though be prepared for the Berliners flock here to beat the heat. Recent renovation efforts continue to improve the city, one example being the revamped Museum Barberini: a city palace that's been turned into a renowned art museum. — ZS

Best for: Innovative minds. More than 30 universities and research institutes have attracted incubators such as the SAP Innovation Center and the Volkswagen Group Future Centre.
What it needs: Quicker public-transport links to nearby Berlin.
Leisure spots? The nearby lakes are plentiful and gorgeous.

Basel, *Switzerland*

Basel is known in the cultural and luxury worlds for Art Basel and Baselworld but the city is vibrant year-round. Bordering Germany and France, it has a European panache that mixes these neighbouring influences, best reflected in the city's museums and architecture; a bike trip around the centre will reveal many feats by the native power firm Herzog & de Meuron. Meanwhile, a prominent pharmaceutical and med-tech sector has made the city a life-sciences hub, and the canton is the most business friendly in already business-friendly Switzerland. Moreover, its attempts to be the first city in the country to introduce paternity leave is proof of its progressive spirit. — ZS

Best for: Hosting a party. When the private jets arrive for the major shows, the doors to swanky mansions and world-class restaurants open.
What it needs: A bike-sharing system to complement its world-class public-transport network.

Chiang Mai, *China*

Feeling the most remote of all the cities in Southeast Asia, Chiang Mai is set against a mountainous backdrop in northern Thailand. With its centuries-old temple stupas and moats, as well as floating markets, it has a relaxed vibe and a creative set shaking up the design, hospitality, culinary and arts scenes. Young Thais fed up with busy Bangkok are establishing small businesses here and blossoming. Further infrastructure is still required for better office space and public transport but new developments can draw upon skilled artisans, architects and local materials. If Chiang Mai continues to balance the old and new, it will be a benchmark for other cities in developing nations. — ZZ

Good education? Of 12 universities here, Chiang Mai University is notable for its fine-arts faculty.
Best for: Food, from street stalls to fine dining.
What it needs: Better public transport. Dense Bangkok has shown what's possible in Thailand.

Victoria, *Canada*

British Columbia's capital, located on Vancouver Island, has long been seen as a little sleepy. But that is changing thanks, in part, to a thriving nascent technology economy and a growing number of young people defecting from nearby Vancouver, where the cost of living on the mainland is soaring. The city's temperate climate, proximity to the Pacific Ocean and rich cultural life (downtown's Munro Books, one of Canada's best independent bookshops, was co-founded in 1963 by Nobel prize-winning writer Alice Munro) are reason enough to move here. — WK

Best for: Outdoor enthusiasts. The Pacific Ocean makes it perfect for swimming and kayaking, while surf breaks are plentiful. There's lots of hiking and three hours north of the city is Mount Washington, Vancouver Island's best ski spot.
What it needs: More housing stock to improve affordability.
Distance to nearest airport? It's 26km to Victoria International.

San Sebastián, *Spain*

This beautiful Basque seaside city may harbour some of Spain's highest housing costs but the rebound effect seems to have lured regional creatives – many of whom have been won over by the beaches, fiercely respected food traditions, world-renowned film festivals and art spaces – to activate other areas of the city, such as the Gros district. Clean and calm, San Sebastián stands as testament to what can be achieved once violent conflicts are resolved and people have common success to share. — LA

What it needs: Cheaper housing. While it was surpassed this year by Ibiza, housing is still more expensive than in Madrid or Barcelona.
Best for: Foodies. San Sebastián has one of the highest concentrations of Michelin stars in the world.
Life expectancy? The region of Gipuzkoa (of which San Sebastián is the capital) has one of the highest life expectancies in Europe: an average of 80 years for men and 86 for women.

Eindhoven, *Netherlands*

Eindhoven locals (even city officials) are quick to admit that their city isn't the prettiest place in the world (or even in the Benelux) but what this small city lacks in beauty, it makes up for in opportunity. Put on the global business map as the home of Philips, the city prides itself on an economy based around innovation. There's a concerted effort to support start-ups and the creative industries – plus an increasing number of students from the respected Eindhoven Academy – are choosing to stick around upon graduation. The city's also undergoing an architectural revamp, masterplanned by MVRDV's Winy Maas and featuring a tree-laden skyscraper by Italy's Stefano Boeri. — NSG

What it needs: As with most cities in the Netherlands, it has great late-night offerings but not a lot going on for early risers.
Best for: Starting up. With Philips manufacturing globally, its old sprawling factory spaces provide ample room for entrepreneurs.
Spot to swim nearby? In a forest beyond the perimeter of the city you'll find Duynenwater Beach.

Bath, *UK*

Close to London and on the right side of Heathrow Airport (and closer still to Bristol Airport), the world never seems too far away from the pretty streets of Bath. You may have to strain your neck over tourists to see the city's Roman remains but there's plenty to enjoy within charming 18th-century buildings, theatres, museums and thermal spa. The city is nestled in the southwest of England, with excellent access to wild swimming spots and cycle routes. — NPO

Best for: Education. The city has five independent schools, a large number of "outstanding" state schools and two respected universities.
What it needs: The city's charm is its quaint English aesthetic but this has been a hindrance in generating a vibrant nightlife and cosmopolitan start-up culture.

Aalborg, *Denmark*

Denmark's fourth city boasts kilometres of cycling lanes, a renovated harbour front and its own university, which attracts thousands of students and contributes to the city's bustling nightlife. Its cultural offerings are strong and a culinary scene is slowly flourishing. However, poor rail and flight connections and a rather weak global outlook, not helped by the government's decision to cut the number of English-language university programmes, mean there is still room for improvement. — GDE

Best for: Design appreciators. The Utzon Centre and the Alvar Aalto-designed museum alone make this city an exciting destination.
What it needs: A more diverse and international environment and better connections. Most international flights connect via Copenhagen.
Cycle-friendly? Yes. We are in Denmark, after all.

Honourable mentions

Wiesbaden, Germany: Has close connections to Frankfurt Airport, wonderful housing stock and a laidback lifestyle but was slightly too large to be cast as "small". But well worthy of your consideration.
Trieste, Italy: This warm, coastal city, close to Venice and filled with historic architecture and excellent eating options, doesn't quite offer enough work opportunities. But it certainly delivers in terms of quality of life.
Haarlem, Netherlands: Adjacent to Amsterdam, this felt a little too much like a suburb of the Dutch capital. But it's this proximity, balanced with a more relaxed version of canal-side living, that gives this small city its appeal.
Annapolis, USA: A push from some US staffers to give this Washington commuter city a look-in for our list was quashed when we learned how bad the traffic was when trying to get from the beautiful bay destination into the capital.
Salzburg: A few more night-life options and attractions beyond the tourist trail might be all this Austrian city needs to be competitive. — NSG

Good Design Induces Resonance

The Good Design Award has been organized annually by the Japan Institute of Design Promotion since 1957 to discover and share exceptional design and encourage further innovation. The Good Design Award defines "good" design as that which has the power to induce "resonance" to involve one's surroundings and suggest some solutions to social issues. This year, 1,420 works were selected from 4,722 entries from all over the world. Here are the Good Design Award 2019 Finalists that represent the very best of this year's entries.

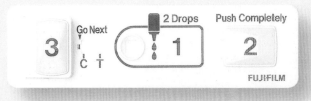

Good Design Award 2019 Finalists

① **[GRAND AWARD]**
Rapid diagnostic kit for tuberculosis
Photographic-development technology enables prompt, inexpensive diagnosis for tuberculosis in emerging nations
Fujifilm Corporation

② **Ontenna sensory device**
Clip-on device converts sound into 256 levels of light and vibration to permit communication across hearing impairments and language barriers
Fujitsu Limited and Fujitsu Design Limited

③ **Gacha self-driving bus**
Community transport option overcomes challenges of autonomous driving in various weather conditions
Ryohin Keikaku Co., Ltd.

④ **"Ever-changing" Ginza Sony Park**
Recreational spot developed on former site of Sony Building offers evolving palette of attractions in upscale shopping district
Sony Enterprise Co., Ltd. and Sony Corporation

⑤ **Igoku community program for geriatric support**
Innovative outreach facilitates socially engaged lifestyles for live-alone elderly, including those who suffer from dementia
Igoku Editorial Department, Iwaki City

GOOD DESIGN AWARD

www.g-mark.org

Drake's

REUSABLE PACKAGING.

RePack
originalrepack.com

OUTSIDE THE BOX

It may now be standard to refuse a plastic bag at
the supermarket but with e-commerce on the rise,
that's only the tip of the iceberg when it comes to the
problems caused by the disposable-packaging industry.
We meet the people with solutions.

PHOTOGRAPHER *Tony Hay*

Online shopping means the packaging market is exploding: it was worth $850bn in 2017 and is predicted to reach $1trn by 2023. But what about the eco-credentials of all the boxes, bags and stuffing accompanying all those purchases? And can companies still communicate their brand's values while being more sustainable? From mushroom moulds to intelligent boxes, we look at how people are rising to meet the challenge. — (M)

I.
The big player
Boxing clever

We're at the Stora Enso packaging factory in the Finnish town of Lahti. The Swiss-made Masterflex flexographic printing-press huffs and puffs as a steady flow of brown corrugated board is fed into the machine. It cuts it into shape and prints the customer's brand identity on it in colourful high-definition, before spitting it out again. A package is born.

"When I joined 11 years ago I could not have imagined that one day we would

> **The amount of cardboard shipped in one day would cover the distance from Brussels to Amsterdam**

achieve this precision and print quality," says production manager Roope Laaksonen, inspecting the final product. That's not the only change that he has witnessed: Nordic paper companies such as Stora Enso were among the largest in the world until digitalisation forced them to rethink their strategy. In a region where much of the land is covered in forest, a renewable and ecological source of raw materials, packaging was the solution.

Leading the charge is Stora Enso. The Finnish paper behemoth employs 26,000 people in 30 countries worldwide and had a 2018 turnover of €10.5bn. The Lahti site is now the largest packaging factory in Scandinavia, churning out 230 million products a year. The amount of cardboard shipped out of the factory in one day would be enough to cover the distance from Brussels to Amsterdam (more than 200km).

"A decade or so ago, 70 per cent of Stora Enso's turnover came from paper but it accounts for less than 30 per cent now; packaging has grown from 28 per cent to about 40 per cent," says Vesa Penttinen, business-development manager for the company's packaging division. Key to this growth is

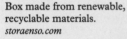

Compostable jiffy
bag made from corn.
betterpackaging.com

Box made from renewable,
recyclable materials.
storaenso.com

Opaque compostable jiffy bag in
two sizes. *betterpackaging.com*

**I'M
A REAL
DIRT BAG**

I'M A comPOST™ PACK

Extra-strong
canister made
entirely from
recycled paper.
nagelpaper.com

Fully recyclable
paper-based
insulator for
perishable goods.
temperpack.com

Compostable
seal-close bag.
tipa-corp.com

Styrofoam alternative made
from water-soluble cornstarch.
greencellfoam.com

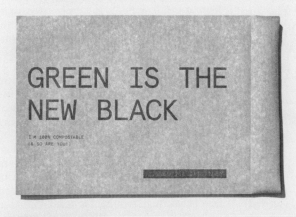

GREEN IS THE
NEW BLACK

I M 100% COMPOSTABLE
(& SO ARE YOU!)

Compostable envelope
for Stella McCartney.
tipa-corp.com

Cardboard
box that can
be reused as
an old-school
Japanese toy.
kami-sumo.
thepack.co.jp

the firm's push towards more innovation in sustainability. Its product line, for example, includes wood-based biocomposites that can replace plastics in cosmetics packaging and be used for renewable and recyclable leak-tight packaging for the food industry. Items designed specifically for e-commerce feature easy resealing for hassle-free returns.

Yet pleasing its clients has required a tricky balancing act: as well as being functional and cost-efficient, packaging also needs to look good. Up on the factory's second floor, designer Outi Honkavaara is busy working out this conundrum for a box that will contain plant seedlings. "Our customers want the packaging to reflect their brand more than ever before," she says.

Sustainable packaging is not just about the right materials or recycling after use. It is also about ensuring maximum efficiency and reducing waste, particularly when it comes to perishable goods. "Soon our packages will be able to sensor what is inside, what the temperature is and how much oxygen there is," explains Juha Maijala, deputy head of intelligent packaging at the company's innovation centre in Helsinki. "Just think about what this can achieve, for instance, in the food industry." — PB

2.
The specialists
Bio-packaging

In 2007, Eben Bayer and Gavin McIntyre started a company based on something most people wouldn't think twice about, something hidden under woodpiles and on tree trunks: mycelium. It's a living organism comprising the cobweb-like roots of fungi that, when combined with agricultural byproducts such as woodchips or cornstalks can be grown into a durable, biodegradable material. It can then be used for any shape desired, from packaging for a wine bottle to protective corners for a TV. "It's able to perform like a plastic during its life cycle," says

Bayer. "Then it actually breaks down and can be returned to the earth as a nutrient."

Today Ecovative Design, which is based in Green Island, New York, is capable of producing 900,000kg of mycelium per year. Customers include Ikea, Dell, and New York-based lighting firm Rich Brilliant Willing. Such eco-friendly products were once too expensive for upstart brands but today they are cost competitive; the firm was able to make custom packaging for direct-to-consumer probiotic firm Seed, despite a modest first order. "The brand is about sustainability so our packaging helps them tell a story that they feel strongly about: protecting both your body and the Earth," says Bayer.

Green packaging hasn't always made a hot sales pitch. In 1997, Tim Colonnese co-founded KTM Industries, a Michigan-based manufacturer of what he called Green Cell Foam: a Styrofoam replacement made of cornstarch for cushioning fragile items. The product is water-soluble so it can be poured down the drain; it also requires 70 per cent less energy to produce and creates 80 per cent less greenhouse gas than conventional foams. The product was released in 2002. "All we heard were crickets," says Colonnese.

By 2010, KTM was on the cusp of bankruptcy. Then, due to a combination of clever business decisions and sustainability rising on the consumer agenda, things started picking up. "Now corporations are hopping on the bandwagon, saying, 'We're getting lots of blowback from our customers and shareholders – we need to be doing better things for the environment,'" says Colonnese. He expects 50 per cent growth in sales in 2020 and again in 2021. "We have yet to scratch the surface," says Colonnese. "If we can make this locally available in more markets – in North America, Europe, Australia – this could be a billion-dollar company."

Both Bayer and Colonnese are focused on making their products widely available. Ecovative Design is licensing its technology to entrepreneurs, while KTM is opening a

> "The first thing we did was remove all the innards from our shirts. Now they're just beautifully folded"

manufacturing facility on the West Coast of the US to avoid lengthy shipping distances and meet growing demand. "It's been a long time coming," says Colonnese. "I've been at this for 22 years and thank God we stuck around, because now people are truly interested in what we're doing." — WK

3.
The industry approach
Experiential unboxing

Fashion pollutes. It's the second-most environmentally destructive industry (oil holds firm at number one). In response, sustainability has become an industry buzzword. Labels such as Raeburn, Stella McCartney and Gabriela Hearst are known for their upcycled, eco-friendly materials and it's now easy to get a thoughtfully produced coat and learn the origin of every fibre. Buy it online, however, and you'll know almost nothing about the packaging it comes in – beyond the fact that some of it is single-use plastic and a lot of it appears unnecessary.

As a result it seems packaging lags behind in terms of sustainability – but the reality is more complicated. Take polybags: those thin plastic bags wrapped around individual items of clothing. The challenge of packaging in fashion extends far beyond them but they illustrate the scale and nature of the problem.

The ubiquity of polybags isn't just due to laziness; the clothing industry has spent a lot of time and money trying to find alternatives. Patagonia, which puts millions of dollars into environmental action, decided it couldn't stop using polybags after testing showed that without them, 30 per cent of goods were damaged before they left the factory. Everlane, a US online clothing company whose slogan is "radical transparency", has committed to removing virgin plastic from its supply chain by 2021: it spent months looking for alternatives to polybags. In the end the best it could do was replace virgin plastic bags with recycled ones.

"A garment that's damaged and can't be used has a significant footprint as well," says Bleue Wickham-Burnham, head of sustainability at UK menswear brand Oliver Spencer. "That's the thing about sustainability: there's no straightforward answer."

Wickham-Burnham has spent a lot of time investigating polybag alternatives. Part of the issue is that, surprisingly, plastic packaging can require three times less energy and emit less greenhouse gas in production than alternatives such as cardboard. "We've talked with recycled paper suppliers but from a carbon perspective, plastic is still the lowest-footprint material at the moment," he says.

Many of the materials that consumers feel good about are less environmentally effective than they seem: the cotton tote's carbon footprint, for example, is 131 times higher than that of a single-use plastic bag.

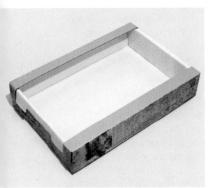 

1 2

Bioplastics – derived from natural materials – are better than standard plastic from a carbon standpoint, according to a University of Pittsburgh study, but deplete more of the ozone and require extensive land use.

Even when everything is designed to have a second life it can still be problematic. High-end online retailer Net-a-Porter now boasts a long list of packaging that is recyclable or biodegradable, including boxes, ribbons, tissue paper, garment-protection bags and shoe dust bags. Yet that's still a lot to manufacture and it will quickly be thrown out.

The most effective solution is no doubt the least technical: just use less. Wickham-Burnham says, "The first thing we did, before even looking at the fabrication of our clothes, was remove all the innards from our shirts: the cardboard, rice paper and plastic in the collar. Now they're just beautifully

3

folded. That's reduced our annual carbon footprint by 36,000kg. The new luxury comes from innovation and ideas – that's what people find interesting."

Have there been customer complaints? "Not one," says Oliver Spencer himself. "And let's say Matches or Mr Porter sends a garment to a customer – he unpacks it, doesn't like it and sends it back. Well, it has to be repackaged again with all that stuff. Now that's not necessary."

Yet it's a dilemma for an industry where a certain quality of packaging has traditionally been part of how luxury brands advertise their value and add to the ceremony of the transaction. People who buy cleaning products on Amazon don't talk about "the unboxing experience"; fashion customers do.

London-based luxury retailer Matches Fashion, for example, has an "eco" packaging option but still offers its signature marble-effect boxes, which are celebrated across social media. The rationale? "Customers expect an experience that reflects the quality and style of the pieces they've purchased," says Jess Christie, chief brand officer. While the company is aware younger customers are "increasingly looking to retailers to support them in reducing their environmental footprints", she says, it also needs to cater to older people's expectations.

Not everyone agrees. "Our customers' relationship to packaging, and to all things ecological, has undergone a notable change," says Tim Sayler, chief marketing officer at Swiss watchmaker Breitling. "Some want only the pouch and others want the watch without anything at all."

It's comforting, and partially justified, to blame giant corporations for polluting the Earth. But when it comes to packaging, we as consumers are a big part of the problem. About 30 per cent of goods bought online are sent back. And each time we buy something in three sizes and return two or have something sent out instead of going to a shop, we're adding to that item's carbon footprint. For fashion to stop being one of the most polluting industries, people will have to shop differently and reassess the sustainability of eco-friendly clothing packaged in a way that undermines the product itself. Consumers will have to decide that, when it comes to fashion and packaging, it's what's inside that counts. — HAN

PUGLIA
UNEXPECTED **ITALY**

*Begin your voyage of discovery through
the delights of Puglian cuisine*

Ph Ekaterina Fedotova

"There's a positive momentum – to put in the work and put things right"

1

GREECE IS THE WORD

Daphne Karnezis REPORTING FROM *Greece:* After suffering an exodus of young talent in the decade following the debt crisis, Greece's slowly improving economy is luring those expats home, armed with the education and determination to lead the country's revival. PHOTOGRAPHER *Bill Georgoussis*

It's a baking-hot September day when we meet Katerina Georgopoulou at the Basil & Elise Goulandris Foundation in Athens. She's in the middle of feverish preparations for the museum's grand opening the following day. The 11-storey building is a significant addition to Greece's culture scene: it has been constructed to house an impressive collection of modern and contemporary art, including Picasso, Van Gogh and Giacometti, plus celebrated Greek artists, and boasts a state-of-the-art auditorium, a library, a shop and a café-restaurant.

"It's been a long time coming," says Georgopoulou, as she shows off the gleaming library with its 6,000-plus art-history titles. She heads up the foundation's educational programmes and, since joining the team in the summer of 2019, often comes here to research content for the museum's

"People are ready for change and not just in politics. Greeks see things differently after the crisis"

print and audio guides. "I remember visiting Athens and walking past the construction site, wondering when it would open. I never expected to be part of the team when the time came to cut the ribbon."

It was a reasonable expectation given that, until a few months ago, Georgopoulou hadn't lived in Greece for nearly a decade. She is one of about 400,000 people – mostly young, educated and from cities – who emigrated as Greece's economy spiralled after the crash of 2008/9. Most went looking for better work opportunities as unemployment soared, reaching a peak of 27.8 per cent in 2013 (and 60 per cent for young people). Georgopoulou, for example, moved to London aged 29 in 2011 and spent eight years working for the Saatchi gallery. Losing many of its best and brightest was a major blow to Greece.

Ten long years – Greece's post-crash timeline:

2009	**2010**	**2011**	**2012**
Global financial crash. Greece's credit rating downgraded due to its government debt.	First bailout of Greece, worth €110bn, agreed by the IMF, the European Central Bank and the European Commission.	Tens of thousands of protesters march to oppose new austerity laws. Prime minister George Papandreou resigns.	A second EU bailout is agreed.

But something is shifting. Georgopoulou is one of a rising number of Greeks choosing to be part of a country that, although still recovering from years of austerity, is starting to find its feet. The economy is growing again, the start-up scene is booming and cultural spaces are breathing life into abandoned buildings. According to recent figures from the Hellenic Statistical Authority, almost 32,000 Greek expats returned in 2017, the highest number in seven years. Could Greece's brain drain finally be ending?

"People are ready for a change and I'm not just talking about politics," says fashion designer Christina Pistofidou, 29. "I think the crisis made Greeks see things differently. There's a positive momentum – to put in the work and put things right."

"Corporate culture is starting to change in Greece. We're not insular any more"

Pistofidou set up her resortwear label, Wéngko Molé, in the UK in 2014 after studying performance costume at the University of Edinburgh. She's in the process of registering the company in Greece, having returned a year ago. "Moving back has been gradual," she says from her Athens studio, which is lined with brightly coloured silk dresses and trousers from her sixth collection. "The printing of our fabrics still takes place in the UK but I've been increasing my collaborations with showrooms in Greece. All the sewing and final production takes place here – everything costs far less." Most of her wholesale orders now come from Greece and she does many of her campaign photoshoots here. "There's so much potential for growth, especially when your product is linked to the summer season," she says.

Pistofidou originally considered moving the company to Greece two years ago but was put off by the amount of red tape involved. "It was a nightmare," she says. "There were so many specifications and prerequisites and also a lot of uncertainty in the country due to the political situation. Now things are more geared towards providing a stable environment for small to medium businesses." Since winning the elections in July, the pro-business government has pledged reforms including corporate-tax cuts and a more streamlined process for setting up shop. "This year, the timing just felt right," adds Pistofidou.

Change is definitely in the air, agrees recent returnee Michalis Rikakis, who left a job at Nokia in 2012 amid an increasingly depressed atmosphere. "Until 2016 there was so much pessimism and perpetuation of negative stereotypes but after 2017 the media coverage calmed down and that helped. Perception can sometimes change reality itself."

Nearly one million jobs were lost in Greece between 2009 and 2015, says the Hellenic Statistical Authority. But that's

2

2013
Unemployment rises to 27.8 per cent with 60 per cent youth unemployment.

2015
Anti-austerity Syriza wins election. PM Alexis Tsipras U-turns and accepts third bailout, making it the largest rescue package ever.

2018
Greece officially exits bailout programme.

2019
Greek economy returns to positive economic growth. Pro-business, centre-right New Democracy party wins the general election.

"Young people need to feel the doors are open for them to return when they want"

3

10 countries and has a production plant in Wisconsin. "People still put their trust in the 'Made in Greece' brand so I was excited to come back and help move the company forwards," says Mandrekas, who's now the company's operations manager. "I'm working on expanding into a new building here in Greece, which will double our capacity."

Things are far from perfect here but lower living costs, a Mediterranean lifestyle and a sense that returnees can contribute to the country's comeback are big draws. According to a recent survey by the Athens-based National Documentation Centre, six in 10 Greeks living abroad want to return. To capitalise on this, the new government appointed Steve Vranakis, former head of Google's Creative Lab in Europe, as Greece's inaugural chief creative officer and tasked him with burnishing the country's image, serving as a special adviser to prime minister Kyriakos Mitsotakis and leading projects to entice back the diaspora.

Independent initiatives to help with the situation are springing up too. Brain Regain was set up in 2019 to connect young Greeks abroad with mentors from different business sectors who can provide advice. "There are people who want to return and don't know where to start. We're trying to connect young people with those who know the market," says Stathis Potamitis, an Athens-based lawyer and member of the non-profit's board.

"I don't think young Greeks should stop migrating to work or study – they should be encouraged to reach their full potential wherever is best," says Georgopoulou, who took her master's in London after completing her studies in Athens, a common practice for Greeks who can afford it. "But I do think that young people need to be presented with enough opportunities to feel that the doors are open for them to return. Brain drain can become brain gain if all the knowledge and skills picked up abroad are redirected back into the country." — (M)

slowly reversing as new companies – particularly in technology, agriculture and tourism – build on the country's growing confidence and find success, pulling back expats in the process. Rikakis, a computer engineer by training, was working for Google in Sweden when he was approached by Workable, a platform offering innovative recruitment software. "It was always the plan to come back at some point but there's no way I'd have left my job if the right opportunity hadn't presented itself," he says. "There are few companies that would have tempted me to return but Workable is one. Corporate culture is starting to change in Greece. We're not insular any more. At Workable we deal with clients worldwide."

On top of coming back to build their own businesses and join promising start-ups, young Greeks are choosing to bolster older firms, often run by their own family. Vasilis Mandrekas, 27, returned in 2016 after six years working and studying in Canada and the US to take his place at his family's 70-year-old dairy business in Corinth, a city in the south. The company, known for its Greek yoghurt, is present in

1.
Christina Pistofidou, founder of clothing brand Wéngko Molé

2.
Michalis Rikakis, vice-president of product, Workable

3.
Katerina Georgopoulou of Athens' Basil & Elise Goulandris Foundation

#1 Private Jet Charter

- ☑ No minimum notice
- ☑ 24/7 Service
- ☑ Anywhere, anytime, any plane

LUNAJETS

fly private at the best price

+41 844 041 844 | lunajets.com

THE REAL THING

Marie-Sophie Schwarzer REPORTING FROM *Munich:* Other trade shows might be more glamorous but Expo Real is where Europe's biggest and most significant deals are cut. We head to Bavaria to peer through the windows of real-estate's future. ILLUSTRATOR *Pascal Blanchet*

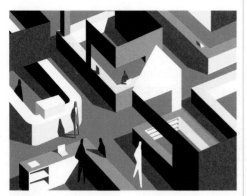

For those in real estate, construction, architecture or anything tangentially related to the property industry, October means one thing: Expo Real. Europe's largest real-estate trade show brings people from all over the world to Munich's Messe München for three days of debate, prospecting and deal-sealing. This year 2,190 exhibitors from 45 countries set up stands across seven halls; they included Invest Stockholm, real-estate and investment firm CBRE, Hyatt hotels and Gina Barcelona Architects.

Between discussing deals, participants chomped Bavarian sausages and supped beer in the autumn sun before rushing off for talks about everything from urban planning to the future of mobility. Some 46,000 people attended – about 4 per cent more than last year – hailing from 76 countries.

More than anything, Expo Real measures the pulse of the industry. This year the outlook was "positive with a note of caution" and there were a few unexpectedly positive signs for the London market. Didn't make it? Fear not. Here is our overview of the best bits and the investment opportunities to watch. — (M)

①

The investment hotspots

What makes a city attractive to investors? Real-estate services firm JLL looked at various criteria to rank the world's leading investment destinations. "Many real-estate investors are targeting cities that are rich in innovation and technology," says Jeremy Kelly, JLL's lead director of global research. Highly connected cities with extensive pools of skilled workers, top universities and a rich culture attract the best talent, he explains.

Brexit has wrought uncertainty in the UK but, long-term, trust in London remains strong. For those looking for more stable investment strategies (with lower yields), Germany, the Netherlands and the Nordics are seen as safe bets. Higher returns (and greater risks) can be found in Ireland, Spain, Poland, Italy and Portugal.

When it comes to predicting hotspots, Kelly bets on "cities that offer high levels of amenities and universities". The marker of a successful city is "one that is adaptable and agile", he adds.

Top investment destinations:
1. London
2. New York
3. Paris
4. Los Angeles
5. Shanghai
6. Seoul
7. Tokyo
8. Hong Kong
9. Washington
10. Chicago

②

The deals

Mipim in Cannes might be where property people party on yachts and network but Expo Real is where deals are actually cut. Here are three that caught our eye.

1. **Long stay:** The UK's InterContinental Hotels Group signed three multiple development agreements to accelerate its growth across Europe. The goal is to add 50 hotels in Europe over the next decade.
2. **Big deal:** Commerz Real of the German Commerzbank made its biggest deal yet by buying dozens of sites from Munich-based insurance firm Generali Lebensversicherung for €2.5bn. The Millennium Portfolio includes 49 office, residential and retail properties in prime German locations.
3. **Nice work:** Germany's Real IS AG bought an office in Australia and is starting to build up a diversified real-estate portfolio there worth up to AU$400m (€245m).

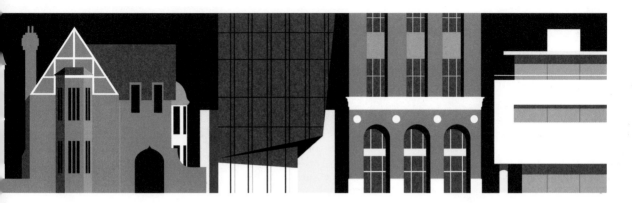

3

The Q&A
Anna Gissler, *CEO Invest Stockholm*

Anna Gissler works on attracting global investment and talent to Stockholm.

Why are you here?
Expo Real is a good place to meet investors from different countries – mainly Germany. We've attended the fair for 15 to 20 years.

More than €111bn in investments are planned for Stockholm by 2040. What developments are you excited about?
Stockholm is one of the fastest-growing cities in Europe. The Meatpacking District, our newest development project, will be an expansion of the city – a place for creativity, culture and start-ups.

What is your aim for 2020 and beyond?
Investing in technology has paid off: we're home to more billion-dollar companies per capita than any region other than Silicon Valley. Our focus on big data centres has attracted firms such as Microsoft and Google. Ultimately our goal is to make the local business environment even better, with a focus on improving quality and work-life balance.

Stockholm developments to watch:

1. **The Meatpacking District**
   Planned opening date: 2030
   Construction of 4,000 homes and 10,000 workplaces has begun. There will also be food, retail and cultural spaces.
2. **Stockholm Royal Seaport**
   Planned opening date: 2030
   As one of Europe's biggest urban developments, this old industrial area will provide at least 12,000 new homes and 35,000 workplaces.
3. **Arstafaltet**
   Planned opening date: 2030
   This 60-hectare greenfield site is being developed into a new city district.

4

The 2020 trends

Germany, France and the UK continue to dominate the real-estate-investment scene in Europe. Housing has established itself as "the new 'sweetheart' of investment in Europe", according to Chris Brett, CBRE's head of EMEA capital markets. It's a trend that he expects to see continue "as demographic patterns and declining levels of home ownership drive demand".

Thomas Westerhof, who runs CBRE's European residential activities, says that housing is a relatively safe bet. It is also evolving rapidly to serve young and old, and provide space to work. "Student housing is gaining ground and senior living is going to have a big growth trajectory," he says. "There's a demand for affordable housing and residential buildings are diversifying in response to that demand. In five years we might start seeing mixed-use spaces with lots of amenities, especially cities with a more mobile and flexible population that is driven by convenience."

5

The future of Expo Real

This year's fair was bigger than ever thanks to the addition of Nova3, a new exhibition hall for businesses focused on how digital products can transform the industry. "We've grown the fair and had a boost of new exhibitors, including those from Malta, asset-management companies from the US and international start-ups," says Expo Real director Claudia Boymanns.

Now the focus is on further expanding Nova3, staying abreast of changes in the industry and developing regional plays, such as a group stand for the Baltics or Nordic countries. Issues discussed here include rapid urbanisation, the revival of inner cities, logistics, affordable living and reducing CO_2 emissions. "Cities are the biggest drivers of change and the interest in exhibiting here is growing," says Boymanns. "I'd like to talk about creating car-free cities and see whether we can find solutions to such issues."

EXPO 2020 DUBAI

From October 2020, Expo 2020 Dubai –
a six-month long event often called the world's
greatest show – will host innovative thinkers
and doers from 192 countries in the hope of
answering today's most pressing questions.

50

questions find 50 solutions

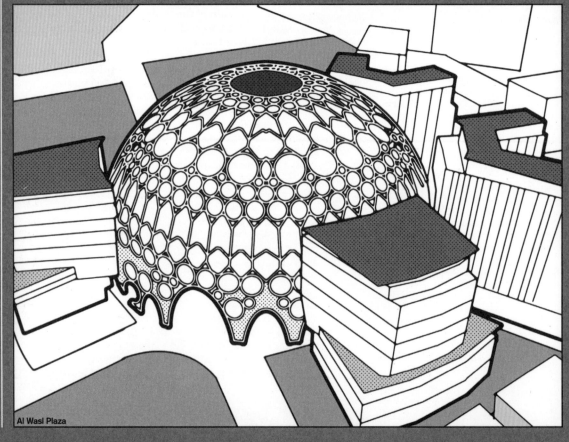

Al Wasl Plaza

What about 2021 and beyond?

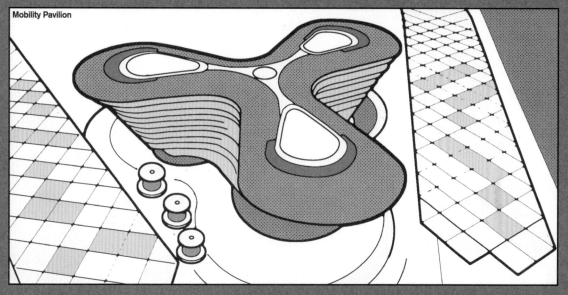

Mobility Pavilion

Sustainability Pavilion

Sustainability

What are some steps Expo 2020 Dubai will take to be sustainable?

Emirati green
Goals include: 85 per cent of all waste treated and diverted from landfill; energy consumption in permanent buildings reduced by more than 30 per cent during Expo; and self-sufficient energy and water usage in the Sustainability Pavilion.

ANIMAL-FREE.
ON MOUNT EVEREST.

SAVE THE DUCK REACHED THE TOP OF THE WORLD,
FOR THE FIRST TIME IN HISTORY
WITHOUT USING MATERIAL OF ANIMAL ORIGIN.

ON MAY 23RD 2019 KUNTAL JOISHER WAS THE FIRST TO CLIMB
MOUNT EVEREST WEARING A 100% ANIMAL-FREE SUIT.

DISCOVER THIS UNIQUE STORY OF EXTREME RESPECT
AND THE COLLECTION INSPIRED BY KUNTAL ENTERPRISE.

SAVE THE DUCK

SAVETHEDUCK.IT

ROLL UP, ROLL UP!

Venetia Rainey REPORTING ON *sun protection:* The planet is getting warmer and urban residents as far north as Sweden are feeling the effects. Don't sweat it: rather than reaching for the air-conditioning, try throwing some shade. PHOTOGRAPHER *Marvin Zilm*

How do you keep cool? Depending on where you live, this might not be a priority right now. But as hotter weather becomes the norm, it's not a question that can be avoided for long. In 2019 the UK experienced its warmest February on record – temperatures reached a balmy 21C – and the previous summer broke records across Europe. Globally, nine out of the 10 warmest years on record have come since 2005.

In many offices, hotels, shops and homes, this kind of weather means one thing: cranking up the air-conditioning. But there is another option for those keen to stay sweat-free without relying on installing unsightly machines: window shades. "We've noticed that growth rates for these are going through the roof in Europe: about 5 to 10 per cent annually," says Alexander Grundhoff, managing director

> "The financial impact of heat on a city can be measured in millions of dollars"

of Germany's Warema International. With 4,400 employees and a turnover of €510m in 2018, Warema Group is the largest supplier of external shades in Europe, selling everything from pergolas to roller shutters. Its sales are historically concentrated in colder countries so its bestselling products have long been geared towards providing insulation and privacy. But over the past 20 years, says Grundhoff, it has seen a marked increase in sales of products for sun protection, particularly exterior Venetian blinds and fabric awnings. "Those products have been grabbing a relatively large slice of the residential market share," he says.

Cooling buildings by preventing sunlight from entering is hardly a new idea. Mediterranean countries have long made use of deep balconies and awnings; southern US homes boast shady porches and verandas; and traditional north African and Middle Eastern buildings feature perforated walls that act as screens. Now the hot weather common in such places is spreading. The planet has warmed by about 1C since 1900, scientists say; and that could rise to 1.5C or even 2C by the end of this century. Heatwaves will become more frequent and last longer. As a result, people in places as far north as Sweden are having to think about ways to cool buildings without changing their architectural vernacular.

Air-conditioning seems like an obvious solution but, as well as looking awful and being noisy, it actually makes the problem worse. In the US, it is used by 90 per cent of homes, accounting for 6 per cent of the country's residential energy use and spewing out 100 million tonnes of carbon dioxide a year. Shades require no energy, have a low carbon footprint and can be used for decades. They also look sharp and provide privacy and security.

Increased interest in such products has been felt along the entire supply chain. "Integrated shading solutions are very Swiss but we now see an increasing demand for it in other countries," says Angelo

Razzino, head of sales at Sky-Frame, a firm based near Zürich that specialises in large high-end frameless sliding doors and windows. "We work with [Swiss shutter firm] Griesser and [customers] get everything from us."

The future looks similarly bright for France's Dickson Constant, a worldwide leader in manufacturing technical textiles. "Our customers are more and more aware that they need to find sustainable solutions to higher global temperatures," says Adrien Derreumaux, who manages the brand's solar-fabrics portfolio. "Shade and sun protection is our number-one market, especially in Europe. In total it accounts for the majority of our business. Within this, our biggest end-product is retractable awnings."

Dickson Constant's direct clients are other businesses, such as Warema. Home owners make up two thirds of final customers, with hospitality and retail companies accounting for the rest. The historic Peninsula hotel in Paris, for instance, was reopened in 2014 after extensive renovations and now features neat green awnings using material from Dickson's Orchestra range. "We still see a lot of potential for further growth, partly because of global warming but also because of the rising costs of energy," says Derreumaux. "Shade and sun protection products are a sustainable way of controlling a building's temperature. There is a greater awareness of the need for that, not just from our end customers but also from the building industry and architects."

Danish developer Ramboll has seen a lot of interest in alternative cooling methods for cities and individuals. It has studied ways to reduce urban heat through its annual Copenhagen Urban Lab, which has run for three years. "In Singapore, for example, they are focusing on greening neighbourhoods and buildings to provide natural cooling," says Christian Nyerup Nielsen, Ramboll's senior director for climate adaptation and landscape.

Keeping cool – a manifesto:

1.
Add loggia balconies that catch the sun less.

2.
Design homes that maximise cross-ventilation.

3.
Use awnings or shutters on any sun-facing window.

4.
Use greenery as much as possible – in the street and on buildings.

5.
Ditch the air-conditioning.

"That includes green façades, roof terraces and green streets. In New York they're going back to older techniques from southern Europe, with much more focus on natural ventilation and all kinds of shading."

When Ramboll works on large-scale projects where air-conditioning is required, it focuses on hybrid schemes. "We design the airflow inside the building and optimise the controls," says Nielsen. "When do you flush air and when do you shade the building? So you can have natural ventilation and then also use ground- or seawater [a sustainable source that is already cooled] for air-conditioning."

Investing in temperature control is about more than fixing a stuffy office. "There are serious health issues at stake," says Nielsen. "There's also the efficiency of the workforce and the effect on infrastructure; the financial impact of heat on a city can be measured in millions of dollars."

As we move into a new, warmer decade, consumers and architects would do well to take advantage of the growing range of options available. Just don't say that you were kept in the dark. — (M)

Timeless *by* Tradition

SieMatic

90 Years of
Kitchen Interior Design
1929 – 2019

SIEMATIC STYLE COLLECTION PURE | siematic.com/showrooms

Modern
Menswear

TALK TO MY AGENT

In an age where self-promotion is the norm and many look for a direct way to success through social media, there's still immense value in having a person on your side who knows how to navigate the industry. We speak to four agents about how their role has changed – and what's on the horizon.

1

PHOTOGRAPHER: MAX BURKHATER

George Lane (THEATRE AGENT)
CAA, New York

Theatre agent George Lane is part of the fabric of New York. In the business for almost four decades, the 67-year-old regularly hashes out deals at a corner table in Manhattan's Gramercy Tavern, about 20 blocks south of his Chrysler Building office at Creative Artists Agency (CAA), where he's been working since 2013. Known for driving a hard bargain, he represents everyone from Alec Baldwin and Sarah Jessica Parker

1.
George Lane
on his red-
hot line

to directors Leigh Silverman and Jerry Zaks (the latter is working on the production of *Mrs Doubtfire* running on Broadway). Unsurprisingly he understands the scene intricately. Best place to start a musical? Easy: La Jolla Playhouse in San Diego. Best client-list ratio? No problem: "Fifty per cent A-list, 25 per cent B-list entering into A-list – and 25 per cent R&D." And there's more… — EJS

"I was born an orphan and adopted. I spent my first five years in Brooklyn and then was part of the great suburban push to Long Island. I then lived in Steamboat

Springs, Colorado, for a couple of years. I wanted to work in entertainment but couldn't find a job so I worked in politics, and actually got a winner in Hugh Carey, who was governor of New York. It was amazing but I needed something with more of a moral centre, so I went into showbusiness.

I started in the mail room at William Morris. It wasn't theatre that drove me; my parents loved theatre but they didn't really take us much as children, nor did I show great interest. But I quickly got to see that it was a place of great collaboration. That was both among the agents and externally, with the actors, the writers, the composers, the lyricists, the directors and the producers – and it was quintessentially New York. I became an agent within four years.

When a writer gives you a script you really are charting a course: in the case of a play, it's 18 months until you get that first production; or, for a musical, three to five years. Once you become a seasoned agent you're working with a group of clients and you know what they're capable of; new talent tends to begin with a recommendation. I'm very comfortable with candidly cold-calling; if I see something amazing I go directly to that person if I don't know them.

The agent is always the go-between: between the talent and the audience but also between the talent and the producer. A big contribution is: 'I think this producer is really right for you, not only for this play but I sense a string of things happening.' You're really relying on your agent to know who's making the decisions and then to execute your deals.

So many projects are based on movies now. When I began in this business it was really about stage to screen – the balance has swung. Normally studios and film producers have a certain number of rights, so in order to take a movie and make it a play or a musical you have to acquire them. Usually the rights are jointly held

"Theatre is a place where you struggle to make a living but you can make a killing"

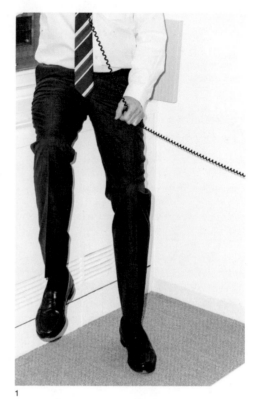

1

1.
He may take calls in his office but much of Lane's business is carried out at the Gramercy Tavern

2.
Janet Carol Norton in her Century City office

by the screenwriter and the producer or the studio. So that's why so many studios have gotten into this business: because they say, 'We already have the rights anyway – why are we licensing to people? We should do it ourselves.' Take a big hit like *Moulin Rouge*: 20th Century Fox has certain rights; Baz Luhrmann has certain rights. Carmen Pavlovic from Global Creatures, the producer, spent seven years putting them all together.

For the individual, theatre is a place where you struggle to make a living but you can make a killing. It's a struggle to make a living as a playwright but the full exploration and exploitation of the rights is highly remunerative. We have eight agents in the department and we're constantly on the road and working with talent in the UK, in LA, in the provinces, in New York – elevating their work, putting it together and reconfiguring it in a way that brings opportunities and financial rewards. We're proud of that. I represent artists and I look to value-up their rights. If it weren't for them we wouldn't have a business – so that's where I stand."

Janet Carol Norton (TELEVISION AGENT)
ICM Partners, Los Angeles

Janet Carol Norton is co-head of the television production department at ICM Partners. For more than 20 years she has represented producers, line producers, production executives and producer-directors working on scripted television, both in the US and abroad. Her roster of clients includes professionals who have worked on shows such as *Homeland, Stranger Things, Veep, How to Get Away with Murder, The Big Bang Theory* and *The Man in the High Castle.* She also serves on the board of governors of the Academy of Television Arts & Sciences, which each year presents the Primetime Emmy awards, honouring the best television in the US. Here she gives us a recap of her career and a teaser of things to come. — CCR

"The blending of film and television has impacted our work in a good way"

2

"A good agent doesn't let you in on the magic of what happens behind the scenes or how a client gets a job or an interview. A client gets the culmination of years of trust that you build with the community you're selling to. Buyers are looking to us to have a curated list of who they need. And a client might not see that the reason they got an audition or a script read was due to their agent's relationship with the buyer.

It's my job to introduce television producers to the community, get them work, finesse the interview process, negotiate the job and set them up as best I can. Most deals are struck via a combination of email and phone calls, whereas it used to be done almost exclusively over the phone and lunch. Formats have changed over the years too: there are fewer and shorter seasons. In the past, producers would do a pilot and you'd wait to see if it would get picked up; now it tends to go straight into the series, which means there's much more preparation in getting it right straight away.

The blending of film and television has impacted our work in a good way: there used to be a feeling of being pigeonholed but now it doesn't matter. It gives talent more opportunity and now I have an agenda to get producers paid differently. In TV, producers have an episodical quote, meaning you go into the negotiation agreeing on a fee per episode. But film producers have a weekly quote and because the business of television now is more like film, that should change – the work often involves fewer episodes over a longer period of time. If TV is filmed like the movies, that should be reflected in the pay.

When I started, nearly 20 years ago, I saw a brick wall for women, especially in directing and producing. I had people laugh on the phone when I'd suggest they should add a female producer or editor to their production. That has changed. In our agency, shortly after the Harvey Weinstein scandal, we pledged to have an equal number of men and women on staff by 2020. I now have people calling me to specifically ask about the female directors or producers I represent and that's really exciting.

This is a business where leadership wants everybody to succeed. Because if you succeed then the client succeeds – and everyone around you succeeds too."

Olivia Mayolle (PHOTOGRAPHY AGENT)
Rose Agency, Paris

Olivia Mayolle founded Paris-based talent agency Rose in 2007. She represents photographers, stylists, set designers, art directors and composers. Though she came from a communications background she chose to start her career in photo-editing with an internship at *Vogue*, before moving on to work for various Parisian photography agencies. Of the decision to bring together her own pool of snappers, she says, "I no longer wanted to sell artists who didn't completely match my taste." — AW

"I've always struggled to put into words what draws me to an artist. I need to like the personality – of them as individuals and of their work. And there needs to be a certain elegance in what they do. I get approached by photographers whose work would do well commercially but if their aesthetic doesn't match my sensibility, it's a no. The decision is simple: yes or no. Being demanding is key for maintaining quality.

There used to be famous photographers whose work everyone was familiar with; this doesn't exist anymore. The industry is so fast-paced, with artists coming and disappearing again within two years. As a reaction I'm building long-term relationships with the talent I represent, helping them develop careers. We function like a family, where all artists know each other and no one is in competition. Some people have been with me since I founded Rose 12 years ago, joining me when they only had a few photos in their portfolio. It's great to follow their evolution over time, even if it means that it will take a couple of years until their work starts to sell. It's little steps at first but there's always a thin glass ceiling that you manage to break eventually. It just requires patience. At the end of the day the role of the agent is also a pedagogical one: we have to make clients understand that work of a certain level deserves a decent salary.

1.
Olivia Mayolle and her pooch, Canada
2.
Bernie Cho: reception's better on the roof, they said

Think about the amount of content we see every day, in magazines or on Instagram. How much of it do we remember? There remains space for quality, work that is well crafted and people who understand the importance of giving it time. More and more artists are returning to non-digital ways of working: shooting film and developing their own photographs. Print is making a comeback too. I represent a publisher of artist books, RVB Books, which has recently exhibited at fairs such as Offprint and Paris Photo. It all moves in cycles but a desire for quality will always exist.

I decided to branch out beyond photography, taking on people working in fields such as set design and music for fashion campaigns. They are all interlinked so the move was a smooth one for me – plus it allows me to offer clients a full palette of artists. I'm proud to have started my own agency that exists in this form now. After all these years my favourite thing about my job remains the daily contact I get to have with my artists. It's a relationship built on trust and affection. I know them inside out but, believe me, they know me just as well."

Bernie Cho (MUSIC AGENT)
DFSB Kollective, Seoul

Bernie Cho is president of DFSB Kollective, a music agency founded a decade ago in Seoul. It represents some of the biggest names in K-pop, from Jay Park to Drunken Tiger, and was one of the first South Korean agencies to sign direct deals with iTunes. Cho splits his time between LA and Seoul. At a time when sex and drug scandals have rocked the once squeaky-clean industry, he tells us how K-pop can bounce back – and how physical sales of CDs and records may yet prove to be the way forward. — KTS

"Korean music becoming a worldwide phenomenon that goes beyond the eye candy of the videos or the ear candy of the melodies; it's to do with the industry's business

"We can't just recruit artists on the basis of how much they can record and sell"

model. Many top Korean music companies are part-agency, part-management, part-label so they are fully stacked to do everything from acting as producers to concert promoters. We handle the merchandising and licensing part of artists' careers too. Top Korean music companies are not only doing well in the music charts: they are also excelling on the stock market. K-pop wouldn't be a global phenomenon without this innovative model that merges strategies from East and West.

There was always pressure to look for the next big thing in the boy-band or girl-band space but our job has been made more complicated by the rise of audition-based TV shows. The discovery and development of talent suddenly became all the more compressed: instead of years it now takes months. The pressure to be discovered, trained and – most importantly – succeed has reached a new level. With talent shows the role of a company's artists and repertoire [A&R] flipped from the industry to the fans. The industry is getting hyper-competitive and this puts a lot of stress on everyone. We've begun to see a few cracks in the system. The current scandals [superstar Seungri was accused of procuring prostitutes at clubs in Gangnam; singer Sulli was recently found dead in a suspected suicide] are reflective of the pressure these artists face. It's a cathartic moment and it's forced people to rethink their value system.

What's also proven disruptive is the surge of new social media. The new Facebook is Instagram; the new Twitter is Tik Tok [a short-video app]. We are constantly on our toes, rethinking our strategy and trying to predict the next big platform.

There are a range of revenue streams that we have to exploit to maintain success. We can't just recruit artists on the basis of how much they can record and sell: we need to understand what will help them generate revenue from alternative streams, be it live performance, film or TV. As digitally advanced as Korea is today, we've seen a resurgence of physical music too: Korea is the fastest-growing physical-music market in the world. When K-pop fans buy a CD they're not just buying music but also merchandise. When I started my agency we were big on download and streaming; now we are more focused on physical music than ever."

Hotel Parador de Cuenca, set in a 16th-century former monastery

HERITAGE
Storied traditions

Paradores preserves Spain's heritage so that visitors can see the storied Iberian nation in its best light. The hotel brand's 97 breathtaking properties have played host to kings, clergy and VIPs for centuries; guests have included Japan's late Emperor Hirohito, Stephen Hawking and Madonna. And the Paradores art collection of 9,000 pieces is as good as that at any major museum, from 2,000-year-old Roman artefacts to works by Picasso, Tapies, Dalí and Miró.

HISTORICAL CONSERVATION
Restored marvels

Paradores gives back to Spanish society through its restoration of historically significant buildings – work that has uncovered hidden treasures and long-forgotten stories. Centuries-old palaces, castles and convents have been rejuvenated, protecting the nation's built heritage. This work often spreads beyond the hotel, which provides the impetus for conservation of nearby public buildings and squares.

SUSTAINABILITY
Green goals

With hotels set among Spain's most dramatic landscapes, Paradores places an emphasis on environmental sustainability. All 97 Paradores hotels are powered entirely by renewable electricity, while quality materials are used instead of disposable plastics. Social sustainability is also a priority; Paradores works with communities to meet thier needs, attracting new residents and visitors in the process.

Visit parador.es

PHOTOGRAPHER: RODRIGO PIEDRA

If you've ever been to a jazz-*kissa* in Tokyo – listening bars where vinyl comes first and conversation second; where the light is low and the whiskey potent – you'll know no other venue can match its impossibly cool atmosphere. Off the success of a few such clubs for audiophiles – from London's Spiritland to Hong Kong's Potato Head – entrepreneurs have decided to export the Japanese model to their own countries. The idea seems to be reverberating nicely so we've pinned down three examples to chart the rising fortunes of the *kissa* abroad. — (M)

1.
Blackforest
Buenos Aires

Coltrane and Hancock aficionados in Buenos Aires finally have an outlet for their passion: the city's – and nation's – first listening bar. Sharing quarters with smart bookshop Falena in Chacarita, Blackforest has taken over the basement to create a temple to jazz on vinyl.

Finnish transplant Jali Wahlsten had long toyed with the idea of a space for music lovers; then he found out about Japan's jazz-*kissa* and realised that the model already existed. "I thought about creating a venue for listening to jazz that allowed music, rather than the space itself, to be the protagonist," he says.

Wahlsten – who's also behind London's Scandi pastry-maker Nordic Bakery – found a

HIGH FIDELITY

As venues for audiophiles take off in global cities, with a heavy nod to the jazz-kissa of Tokyo, we explore three places where vinyl collections are played on some of the world's best analogue equipment – with strong spirits and wine lists to match.

1.
Unlike many orthodox Jazz-kissa in Japan, lively chatter is allowed at Black Forest
2.
Positive spin

kindred creative spirit in Falena owner Marcela Giscafré and they opened Blackforest in 2018. It was quite a slow start: "Our soft launch lasted seven months," he says, laughing. "But by taking an organic approach we made it our own."

Unearthing rare Altec Lansing speakers and McIntosh amplifiers from an analogue equipment restorer was key; listening to music on these powerful beasts is a novelty for many *porteños*. "They often ask us, 'Now what do we do?'" says Giscafré. The answer: nurse a glass of single-grain whiskey and let the music do the rest. Either Wahlsten or "selectors" (DJs) choose vinyl for Thursday-evening sessions; one Monday a month is dedicated to live performances, a *porteño* touch that diehard *kissa* fans may draw the line at.

The eclectic basement borrows from Nordic and Latin

American aesthetics, including wicker furniture sourced from the Delta and some Persian rugs gifted by the Finnish embassy.

The pair considers Blackforest a work in progress, allowing it to evolve at its own pace. Though as its popularity keeps rising and people are inspired to follow, they may not hold on to nationwide primacy for long. — SMW
Charlone 201

2.
Rhinoçéros
Berlin

"We wanted to do something that wasn't like every other bar in Berlin and the idea of the Japanese jazz-*kissa* combined all the things we love – vinyl, jazz, whiskey and good sound – in one place," says Martina Carl, who co-founded Rhinoçéros in Berlin with her husband Bénédict Berna about two years ago.

An homage rather than a perfect facsimile, Rhinoçéros adapts the concept of Japanese *kissa* for a German audience, replacing the customary whiskey and soda with classic cocktails, a host of spirits and an eclectic selection of wine. "We don't want anyone to come here and think, 'Oh, I'm in Japan,'" says Carl. "We want them to feel like

they are in a very intimate and comfortable space."

With its open fire, low lights and minimal decoration, Rhinocéros's unfussy interior allows the focus to be on the real stars: two wooden Bowers & Wilkins speakers from 1976, a Micro Seiki Turntable from 1981 and an early 1970s Quad amplifier and preamplifier.

Tuesday to Saturday, this vintage soundsystem plays albums

5

from the couple's 800-strong collection of vinyl jazz records to a roomful of interested locals, wine lovers and audiophiles – but the concept really comes alive every second Monday, at the bar's listening sessions. "During these events, it's like a church," says Carl. "Everyone sits in complete silence." For those passionate about music, these events can be almost overwhelming. When Italian fans filled the bar to hear Lucio Battisti's South American-inspired masterwork *Anima Latina*, some were so taken by the experience that, according to Carl, "tears were streaming down their faces". — CST
rhinoceros-berlin.com

4

1.
Not just whiskey: wine is surved at Black Forest too
2.
On a roll
3.
Hey, Mr DJ, put a record on
4.
Micro Seiki DQX-500 turntable

5.
Suitable accompaniment
6.
Martina Carl (left) discussing the next tune

6

3.
Public Records
New York

"You can have a great bar and the music is very pedestrian – or it's the other way around," says Francis Harris, one of the partners at Public Records. Billing itself as a social space, hi-fi bar and sound room, it is the result of Harris and his collaborators "bringing the two worlds together". It opened earlier this year in a vast red-brick building from 1912 – which mirrors the architecture of the Gowanus Canal pumphouse opposite – and is one of the driving forces in a rapidly changing neighbourhood. Where there was once a church pipe organ restoration outfit and a vintage guitar shop, today this space is more whitewashed walls and soft lighting meets eminently noticeable (and very impressive) audio equipment.

Alongside a small record shop featuring choice vinyl, a magazine kiosk and a coffee machine, there is a larger, high-ceilinged space where cocktails are being mixed. At the other end of the room a DJ plays anything from ambient or techno to Pink Floyd – it's a notch above background music without making it feel like a club. "We have a really strong regular community," says fellow partner Shane Davis. "It's become a home for a lot of people."

While Public Records may not uniquely lure music lovers, the space is clearly put together by people who are passionate about it. First there are the bespoke Ojas speakers with their DIY aesthetic, made down the road in Clinton Hill. And then there's the beautiful custom-made mixer from London's Isonoe at the DJ booth. The icing on the cake may well be the Sound Room, a separate area decked out with plywood and a raised stage. With programming Wednesday to Sunday, events here cover everything from live music to "first listens" of new albums, followed by a Q&A (as was the case recently with FKA Twigs).

While clearly related to the *kissa* model, Harris argues that his venue is much less precious than its Japanese counterparts. "This is more democratic," he says. "You don't have to be a DJ to come in!" — EJS
publicrecords.nyc

Belvita

LEADING WELLNESSHOTELS
SÜDTIROL

brandnamic.com | Photo: Belvita-Hotel Panorama Wellness Resort Alpen Tesitin (Harald Wisthaler), Belvita-Hotel Alpin & Spa Resort Schwarzenstein (Klaus Peterlin)

BELVITA – THE BEST HOTELS IN THE ALPS

Luxurious wellness, culinary delights, and premium service – the Belvita Leading Wellnesshotels Südtirol offer guests from near and far an exclusive pampering holiday with 100% quality in all areas. Nestled in the most scenic locations of South Tyrol, the family-run 4-star superior- and 5-star spa hotels are the go-to destination for exclusive holidays in Italy's northernmost region. Whether you are a gourmet, an active holiday maker, or a relaxation seeker – you've come to the right place with Belvita!

BELVITA LEADING WELLNESSHOTELS SÜDTIROL
Italy . T +39 0473 499 499
wellnesshotels@belvita.it . www.belvita.it

1

CALLING THE SHOTS

Alexei Korolyov REPORTING FROM *Budapest:* Its émigrés helped to shape the global film industry and now the country itself is becoming a cinema and TV production hub. So how is Hungary earning its starring role as the Hollywood of Europe? PHOTOGRAPHER *Gregor Hofbauer*

It's noon in the woods outside Budapest and a ragtag army of Germanic tribesmen has just finished fighting a crack Roman legion. This was only a skirmish but soon a proper assault will begin: the famous Battle of the Teutoburg Forest in 9AD, a nation-defining moment for the Germans and the focus of hotly tipped new Netflix series *The Barbarians*. The original setting of that clash still exists: said forest is in Germany's Lower Saxony, more than 1,100km northwest of here. As it's now a protected national park, filming there would have been a logistical and financial headache. In Hungary, however, the whole operation is rather smooth.

"When we were shooting *A Good Day to Die Hard* in 2012 we closed down a motorway for three days straight," says Mihaly Korom, head of productions at Origo Studios, Hungary's largest film studio,

2

which is working on *The Barbarians* today. "Can you imagine something like that in Paris, for example? There would be a revolt."

This laissez-faire approach to using public space is one of many reasons why, over the past few years, foreign productions have flocked to Hungary. Origo was founded in 2010 and its fortunes have risen with the city's cinematic clout. Based on the outskirts of Budapest, it's home to nine soundstages, warehouses and backlots spread over an area as big as 31 football pitches. It employs 50 people on a permanent basis but that number can balloon to several hundred depending on the scale of the production. Origo's recent titles include multimillion-dollar blockbusters *47 Ronin*, *Blade Runner 2049*, *Inferno* and *Atomic Blonde*, the 2017 thriller starring Charlize Theron.

Yet there are many other factors behind the country's appeal to film-makers. "[People here] have high professional standards, are fluent in English, and have the skills and manpower," says Barbara Eder, Austrian-born director of *The Barbarians*, during a short break from bloody combat. Perhaps the biggest boon, though, is Hungary's huge tax rebate on all films, which was introduced in 2004 (it excludes films with adult content, a genre that's flourished in Hungary despite the less favourable tax terms). The rebate was bumped up to 30 per cent in 2018; as a result, Denis Villeneuve's upcoming *Dune*, also produced with Origo, made record savings of €24m.

Over this period the number of foreign productions has rocketed – the industry now brings about €360m a year into state coffers. Add to this the relatively cheap labour and the architectural versatility of Budapest (which has variously been made to look like Paris, New York and Copenhagen) and you'll see why the city has earned its reputation as the Hollywood of Europe.

Hungarians will proudly tell you there's a long history connecting the nation to the global film industry. Many founders

The film industry now brings about €360m a year into Hungary's state coffers

of Hollywood's biggest production houses were either born in the then Austro-Hungarian empire or came from immigrant Hungarian families who moved to the US in the 1900s. Adolph Zukor, the co-founder of Paramount, was one of them, and so was William Fox of 20th Century Fox fame. The birth of Hungarian-based production powerhouses has furthered this tradition and finally made returns for the country's reputation – and its bottom line.

"This makes Hungarians proud," says Origo Studios CEO Marta Fekszi Horvath. "It supports whole sectors of the economy: hotels, restaurants, spas, car rentals, taxi services, construction firms – you name it." The country's cinematic credentials have helped domestic film production too. Hungarian director Laszlo Nemez's debut, *Son of Saul*, was shot on home ground and won an Oscar, a Golden Globe and a Bafta.

Located in the countryside just outside Budapest, Korda Studios is another major winner in Hungary's lucrative silver-screen industry. Its vast exterior set spaces have been used for titles such as *Hellboy II: The Golden Army*, Will Smith thriller *The*

Previous page:
1.
On set with 'The Barbarians'
2.
Getting into character

This spread:
1.
Extras taking a break
2.
Just like the real thing
3.
Barbara Eder, director of 'The Barbarians'
4.
A New York street mock-up, as seen in 'Hellboy II: The Golden Army'

3

4

1.
Origo CEO
Marta Fekszi
Horvath
and head of
production
Mihaly Korom

2.
Light and grip
equipment line
the shelves

3.
An empty
lot at Origo
Studios won't
stay that way
for long

4.
Editing
facilities
at post-
production

Gemini Man, space drama *The Martian* and Showtime period series *The Borgias*. The sets are so elaborate that some of them have been turned into open-air museums. "Everybody who comes here says that Hungarian craftsmen are the best," says Korda's Richard Sandorfi, standing in the studios' visitor centre. Sets can take years to build so, instead of tearing them down, producers sometimes prefer to redecorate and add props. The Renaissance city created for *The Borgias*, for example, was adapted for a subsequent sci-fi production.

Requests to film at Origo and Korda pour in year round but the busiest months are from March to November. At the time of writing, all six of Korda's soundstages are in use for a large international production, while Origo's lots are almost full – and demand for studio space is growing. "Because of the global switch towards video on-demand, clients such as Netflix have to produce content all the time," says Origo's Korom. "Most of our business these days comes from that."

But as business booms is there a danger that Budapest's cinematic success could have unwelcome repercussions? Part of the city's appeal for film-makers is its less salubrious areas, which allow it to stand in for Cold War Berlin or modern-day Moscow. Will the industry's rising revenue change it beyond recognition? Barbara Eder doesn't think so. "Budapest is being renovated and new neighbourhoods are being built but you will always be able to find special corners that tell a story," she says, as the cast of *The Barbarians* start another scene. "In fact I wish I were shooting in the city right now – but I'm afraid my series is set in the wrong time period." — (M)

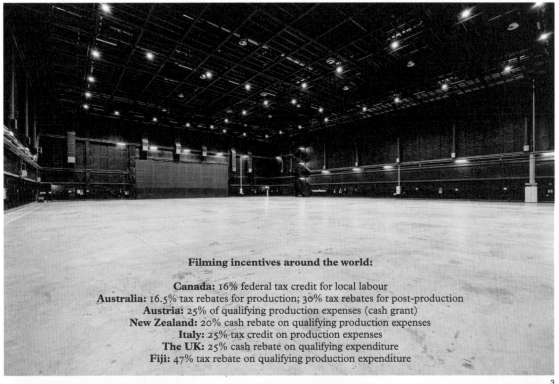

Filming incentives around the world:

Canada: 16% federal tax credit for local labour
Australia: 16.5% tax rebates for production; 30% tax rebates for post-production
Austria: 25% of qualifying production expenses (cash grant)
New Zealand: 20% cash rebate on qualifying production expenses
Italy: 25% tax credit on production expenses
The UK: 25% cash rebate on qualifying expenditure
Fiji: 47% tax rebate on qualifying production expenditure

3

4

© Delfino Sisto Legnani

ART INSPIRES TECHNOLOGY
TECHNOLOGY COMPLETES ART

The form and function of the LG SIGNATURE OLED TV reveal themselves in a collection
of minimal forms, shown in perfect harmony. As the world's first and largest 8K OLED TV,
it features an immersive 88" canvas for unforgettable picture quality.

LG SIGNATURE
OLED 8K

LOOSEN UP IN LOS ANGELES

When life gets busy, make sure there's time for staying
in and slowing down with the LG SIGNATURE OLED 8K.

Welcome to Hollywood – indoors and out. There's no place better than Los Angeles
to enjoy the world's first 88-inch OLED 8K. With an 80 watt output (the highest of any
LG TV) and 33 million pixels to the screen, it means that you won't miss a thing when
you're watching the latest blockbuster. Meanwhile the handcrafted aluminium stand
will catch the eye of any design-savvy director who comes knocking at your door.

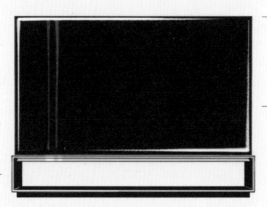

This TV stand
is made from
top-of-the-range
aluminium to
enhance rigidity
and make for a
flawless design.

The world's largest
OLED 8K provides
an ultravivid picture
and powerful
sound.

A durability test
places the TV under
harsh conditions
for 168 hours to
ensure perfect
performance.

LG SIGNATURE ×

LET'S MAKE IT A GOOD ONE

A new year is the time for bringing out your best stationery and writing a list. Ours is a rundown of things that are set to make life better in the coming year, whether it's a clever new business or a cultural opening, a flicker of improvement in a beleaguered metropolis or a city hall doing great things with public transport. We've also added some suggestions, from how to sleep well to how to improve on a gin and tonic. Here's to a hopeful 2020.

ILLUSTRATOR *Massimiliano Aurelio*

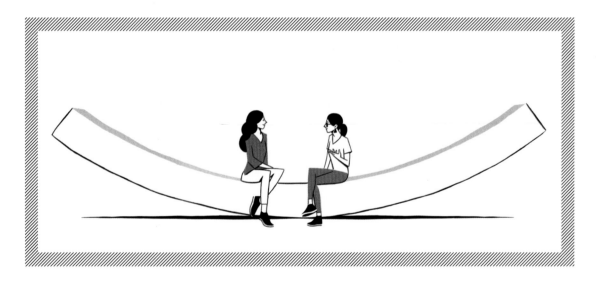

1.

A sociable seat, *New York*

The knotted gun sculpture at the UN headquarters plaza is an artful reminder of the organisation's aims – and since autumn 2019 it has been kept company by a bench designed by Norwegian firm Snøhetta. The inspiration? A quote from Nelson Mandela and the idea that "the best weapon is to sit down and talk". The raised edges and curved design of the simple seat makes sitters gravitate inexorably towards one another, enabling conversation and pushing people to recognise their closeness rather than just their independence. "Our aim was to create an object that was relatable to everyone yet effectively delivering the message of the project's vision: to resolve conflicts through dialogue," says Marius Myking, director of product design at Snøhetta. It's a fitting idea for the site. In 2020, urban-planners and architects should bear in mind how buildings and the built environment shape the behaviour of the people who use them. — AW

2.
A private view
Paris

Pinault Collection, which opens in Paris's Bourse de Commerce in June 2020, is the latest Paris museum to challenge the notion that only the state should show major artworks. — TLE

3.
Streets for people
New York

In 2019, New York banned cars on Manhattan's 14th. So far the experiment has been a success: instead of the chaos many critics feared, bus speeds have increased by about 30 per cent and the surrounding area is noticeably quieter. — CCR

4.
Proper food shopping
Switzerland

The Swiss Coop is showing how to mingle online and physical retail with Fooby. It hosts online cookery classes and recipes but also has a buzzing shop in Lausanne, brimming with fresh food, cookbooks and kitchen kit. — JAF
fooby.ch

5.
A real looker
Global

Sony's RX1R II compact camera is a professional-standard digital snapper. Unlike your phone it won't buzz or ring – or wrangle you for updates. — JAF
sony.com

6.
A light touch
Germany

Axel Meise, founder of German lighting brand Occhio, saw the need for different rooms to have their own solutions and produced lighting systems that could be adapted according to their setting. Bad lighting is bad for our health; 2020 is the year to throw some shade. — HU
occhio.de

7.
Manners on the move
Global

Public transport is undeniably a good thing but airlines, train and bus firms need rules for use. Here are some for starters: no filming or photographing other passengers, phone calls to be conducted out of earshot and anyone playing music out loud to be swiftly ejected from the vehicle in question. — JAF

8.
Making tracks
Los Angeles

Founded in 2015, Los Angeles-based sportswear brand Lady White Co opened its first shop, on Hyperion Avenue, in 2019. Its clothing can be found in more than 60 stockists, from Stockholm to Kyoto, but it still produces its collection in family-owned factories in Los Angeles. Retail done right: a good brand story and well-made products still sell. — WK

9.
Open kitchen
Copenhagen

Chef Kamilla Seidler, who won acclaim while at Claus Meyer's Gustu in Bolivia, has returned to the Danish capital with Lola, a restaurant that employs people on the fringes of the job market (new immigrants and "young women who are a bit feisty"). Expect a menu of cutting-edge fare with an emphasis on human as well as environmental sustainability. — MB
restaurantlola.dk

Pinault Collection: state of the art and not art of the state

Congestion-easing suggestions from New York

Fooby has a tasty Swiss take on food retail

Sony's compact solution

Occhio is getting the light right

10.
Mix it up
Global

Gin and tonic is so ubiquitous that it's a bit like tea or toothpaste: just a thing in your weekly shop. So what else to put with tonic? Well there's Lillet Blanc, the wine-based aperitif, white port or tequila. You might think the latter a waste of the old rare agave – until it hits your lips in its mixed form. — RB

11.
A local designer
Global

For a house or hotel revamp in the Med, look up Palma-based OhLab, whose work at the Can Bordoy Hotel speaks for itself. Melbourne-based Edition Office is a dab hand with fitting projects into landscapes, while Swedish firm Elding Oscarson shows why Scandi design is still the envy of the world. — JAF
ohlab.net; edition-office.com; eldingoscarson.com

12.
Buildings that last
Byron Bay, Australia

Sydney-based architecture firm Chrofi is behind a new project in Byron Bay, which includes a subtropical rainforest and the stone-built Lune de Sang Pavilion. Materials were either sourced in Australia or recycled, while all the water that's used is ultimately returned to the forest ecosystem. — CSM
chrofi.com

13.
An easy ride
Seattle, USA

City hall has approved the use of regional transit passes on Seattle's Monorail line, integrating it with the bus, train and light-rail system. Riders can now move between services without having to fumble for change; ridership is anticipated to increase by 16 per cent. — NM

14.
Shoes to shine in
Global

In 2019 we've noted that white trainers have become the de facto work shoe of the "creative class" – but not in winter and not forever. John Lobb, Crockett & Jones, Berluti and Brunello Cucinelli are where to go for proper shoes in fine leather and staff who know their stuff. — RB

15.
Arts for minds
Hong Kong

Hong Kong's M+ Museum by Swiss firm Herzog and de Meuron will be built by March 2020, with doors opening nine to 12 months later. The museum will house modern and contemporary art and will be a platform for discourse when the city needs it the most. — KTS

16.
Coast to explore
Istria, Croatia

For a summer free of traffic and tourist tat, try the coast of Istria. Fine virgin olive oil, wine and hospitality are generously served at tables in picturesque towns. — LA

17.
High hopes
Innsbruck, Austria

Innsbruck is home to some of Europe's best ski and winter clothing brands. If you fancy setting up shop in the Alps, call start-up centre InnCubator. See what they've done there? — AKO
inncubator.at

Aiming high: Seattle's monorail

Sydney firm Chrofi has the measure of sustainable architecture

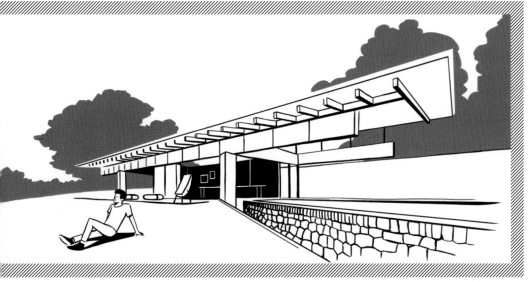

A built-to-last building with rainforest, local materials and communal spaces. The lawn's nice too

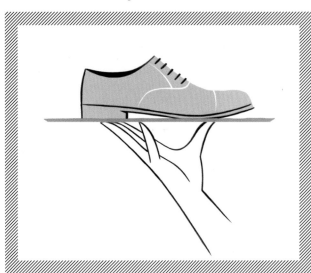

John Lobb's shoes are a step ahead

Oh, go on then. G & T without the G

18.
Trees, please
Los Angeles

Rachel Malarich, Los Angeles' first forest officer, is hard at work to meet the city's goal to plant 90,000 trees by 2021. This will increase the tree canopy by at least 50 per cent by 2028. Here's hoping the idea takes root in other cities soon. — CCR

19.
Plugged-in transport
Canada

NFI Group was founded in Winnipeg in 1930 and is now the leading independent producer of electric buses. Its astute 2019 acquisition of one of the UK's most storied double-decker bus-maker, Alexander Dennis, will expand its reach over the electrification of public transport even further in 2020. Honk, honk. — TLE

20.
A serve of civility
Beirut

If there's one thing that Beirutis do well it's enjoy themselves, despite Lebanon's political strife. Open since 1949 (even during the 15-year civil war), Hanna Mitri in Furn el Hayek serves mastic ice cream and sorbets to long, friendly queues of customers of all stripes. A little of this decency and co-operation will go a long way in 2020. The ice cream's not bad either. — JAF

21.
Bedroom antics
Global

Making a splash in 2020 doesn't only mean a city transport revamp or a new business model. Small, subtle fixes can improve your life and here's something… for the bedroom.

Turn off your phone and invest in an alarm clock – or, better still, a clock radio – and get some real shuteye. — JAF

22.
One stop closer
Paris

After 10 years of redevelopment, Paris's Gare d'Austerlitz is reopening. It's a work in progress but the investment has put the whole area back on track. Cities take note: as King's Cross in London shows, stations can be nice places. — AW

23.
City comeback
Istanbul

Istanbul is under new management with mayor Ekrem Imamoglu. The new airport will be followed by the redevelopment of Galataport, and, after a torrid few years, 2020 should see visitors and investors return. — JCH

24.
Retail done right
New York

While other department stores decline, in 2019 Seattle-based chain Nordstrom opened a New York flagship on 57th Street, grasping that simple things done well work, from customer service to store layout. — EJS

25.
Waste not
Global

It's time to take stock of our wasteful consumer habits. Need a new jacket? Get a well-made one from Venetian tailor Barena. Upgrading the furniture? Invest in a set from Japanese wood specialist Maruni. Make 2020 the year you only buy things worth holding on to. — JAF

Trees in cities are a beautiful thing – just ask LA

Winnipeg's NFI has electrified the market

Beirut knows how to cool off

Remember this? You'll sleep easier without your mobile

Now arriving in Paris's Gare d'Austerlitz: a city train station that isn't terrifying

Un-bearably cute: Kumamon

As Chanel illustrates, there's no reason for building sites to be shabby

26.
Couture construction
Paris

While waiting to unveil a new Parisian home for its *métiers d'art* division in autumn 2020, Chanel has tapped street-art collective Quai 36 to create a series of murals for the fences surrounding the site. The work by German artist Case Maclaim depicts the hands of Chanel craftworkers as they sketch, cut patterns or embroider fabric. Who says construction sites can't be beautiful? — AW

27.
Bear-faced branding
Japan

Do you or your business need a soft-pawed, soft-power leg-up? The charm offensive to learn from for 2020 comes from Japan's Kumamon character (see issue 129 of MONOCLE), a bear whose rosy-cheeked, low-tech, happy-go-grizzly vibes are a lesson in small-scale statecraft. The understanding is that anyone in Japan can use his image for free as long as they namecheck the Kumamoto prefecture of his birth. As a result this rural, volcano-strewn corner of Japan manages to pack a punch that's way above its weight. — RB

28.
Sportswear to sweat for
Global

And Wander, from designers Keita Ikeuchi and Mihoko Mori, has scaled new heights with its Alpine-inspired outdoorswear; for women we'd suggest an acquaintance with east London label LNDR. For shorts we'd advise Californian brand Olivers – and finish the look with French firm Veja's first high-performance trainers. These colourful mesh-topped treads are billed as the first post-petroleum running shoe. — JAF
andwander.com; lndr.uk; oliversapparel. com; veja-store.com

29.
Growing up
Paris

Paris is opening the world's largest urban farm on top of a 15th arrondissement hall; the Agripolis project will also have a bar and restaurant and community allotments for green-fingered city slickers. Fruit and vegetables species will be farmed vertically, both feeding the neighbourhood through vegetable-box schemes and supplying food entrepreneurs. Tasty suggestion. — AW

30.
A rosy future
São Paulo

The Rosewood São Paulo will launch in late 2020. The hotel was designed by Jean Nouvel and will become the centrepiece of the 20th century Cidade Matarazzo complex, Another reason to visit the city in 2020. — MSS
rosewoodhotels.com

CELEBRATE IN ROME

Want to mark the occasion? Grab a bottle of your finest
vintage from the LG SIGNATURE Wine Cellar.

A bottle of the white soave or the red primitivo? Available early next year, the LG
SIGNATURE Wine Cellar has room for both thanks to its multi-temperature control,
which allows every shelf to be individually adjusted. Darkened glass on the InstaView
Door-in-Door protects your bottles from the Roman sun and turns clear with just two
knocks. *Saluti*!

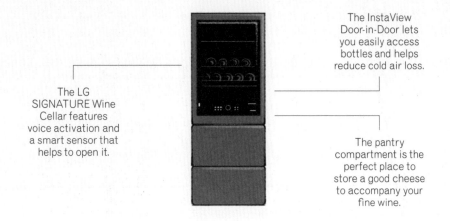

The LG
SIGNATURE Wine
Cellar features
voice activation and
a smart sensor that
helps to open it.

The InstaView
Door-in-Door lets
you easily access
bottles and helps
reduce cold air loss.

The pantry
compartment is the
perfect place to
store a good cheese
to accompany your
fine wine.

OPEN BOOK

Hester Underhill REPORTING FROM *Helsinki:*
The Finnish capital's new public library was the result of an anonymous open competition. The commission points to a smart future for cities seeking to nurture talent while improving their urban fabric.
PHOTOGRAPHER *Carl Bergman*

For the average Finn, a public library is much more than a stuffy spot you visit to borrow a book. Libraries have long offered cosy nooks for readers to escape the harsh, long winters, as well as providing important social centres. "It's more of a village hall I suppose," says Samuli Woolston from ALA, the architecture firm behind Helsinki's new Oodi Library. This addition to the country's 900-strong network of public libraries opened in late 2018 and welcomes 9,000 daily visitors. The building has three floors and houses a cinema, communal kitchen, editing suites, music-practice rooms and workshops kitted out with 3D printers, sewing machines and laser-cutters.

1

It's no wonder the library has been dubbed "Helsinki's new living room"

Previous spread:
1.
Oodi Library

This spread:
1.
Atrium in
Jätkäsaari School
2.
Deputy mayor
Anni Sinnemäki
3.
Exterior of
Jätkäsaari
School
4.
Arto Ollila and
Kuuti Halinen
5.
Teaching space
at the school
6.
Room to learn

You won't find any books until you reach the third floor – and even this isn't the hushed environment of a typical library. A café sits in the centre of this open-plan space, while one end hosts a snug, padded cave where children can sit and have stories read to them by a librarian. It's no wonder the library has been dubbed "Helsinki's new living room".

The library is the product of a century-long architectural tradition in Finland: the open, anonymous competition. Usually any practice can enter these competitions, no matter their level of experience, and they are judged on architectural plans alone. "The National Museum over there: that was the winner of an open competition," says Woolston, looking out of the vast top-floor window over Kansalaistori Square. "Basically all of these buildings around us are: the Parliament building, the Helsinki Music Centre, Kiasma Art Museum."

And it's not always the big-name firms that win. "The young architects often put more of an effort in because for them, it's more important to prove themselves than the established firms," says Anni Sinnemäki, who as deputy mayor of Helsinki is responsible for city-planning and overseeing real-estate developments. "When ALA won in 2013, there were more famous studios participating – ALA were the underdogs."

5

The city's population has grown by more than 10 per cent over the past 10 years and catering to this expansion also helps to create work for Helsinki's architects. "In a city where you build a lot, you simply have more opportunities," says Sinnemäki. "As the city grows it's not only housing that we build but new services like schools and kindergartens."

The latest school to open in the city was designed by young architectural firm AOR. Its winning design is a compact, boxy structure lined with square windows and vast angular balconies overlooking the enormous cruise liners docking in the harbour opposite. Built to accommodate 800

6

children, the building is more than just a new public service for the area: it represents a whole new system of education. In 2015, the year the firm won the competition to design the school, Finland approved a complete refresh of the country's education system. "You can't compare this to all schools in Finland because it's been designed in a really different way," says Arto Ollila, founding partner of AOR.

Lessons now have a more collaborative format, whereby children problem-solve in smaller groups while several teachers take large classes of mixed age groups together. AOR's design had to suit this new system. "The main idea is to have a lot of spaces where children can move around," says AOR architect Kuutti Halinen. "The spaces also needed to be flexible, with ways of adapting for larger and smaller classes."

The school was the first competition won by AOR, which founded its practice only after its design was selected – just a month before two of its three founding members graduated from Helsinki's Aalto University. "It may seem like a huge risk to make an open competition and have some really young architects win without even having an office or any references," says Ollila. "But it's the best thing for cities to do these kinds of architecture competitions because if they ordered such a large number of designs from some big consultant company, it would be super expensive." The system is also a good way of stopping established firms from resting on their laurels. "It keeps the older generation on their toes," says Ollila. "The younger generation often win because they think about things differently and have a fresh perspective on design."

Earlier this year, AOR's founding partner Erkko Aarti was chosen to be on the judging panel for a competition to design a new school in the city of Lappeenranta. The winning design came from AS LL TK: a group of three young architects, the eldest of whom only recently turned 30. The school is for 1,000 pupils, making it one of the largest in the country. "For a young architect, the size is almost overwhelming," says Leo Lindroos, a partner at the firm. "But it's amazing to be able to cut our teeth on a project like this."

Another young practice to get its big break through the open competition system was architecture firm Noan. "Back in 2015 we won a big competition to plan a new region for the city of Tampere, for 25,000 inhabitants; we got work from that for the next two years," says founding partner Lassi Viitanen. When we visit, Viitanen is adding the finishing touches to a smaller-scale project: a remote wooden chapel beside a lake two hours north of Helsinki.

With a small budget, the chapel was commissioned by the local parish and has been constructed mainly by volunteers (one of whom is Viitanen's own father). The result is an elegant space with a tall, vaulted ceiling patterned by curving spruce beams. "This project was my master's thesis," says Viitanen, who since graduating has gone on to work on projects around the country, from a new public pool in Rauma to a church extension in Lieto. "By entering these open competitions you get better and better all the time; you keep yourself sharp and keep yourself designing. Finland's competition culture is something unique and it's really important for us to maintain it." — (M)

1.
Atrium ceiling at Jätkäsaari School
2.
Ceiling of Tervajärvi chapel
3.
Designer Yrjö Kukkapuro's CNC-1 chair at Oodi
4.
The chapel
5.
From l-r: Leo Lindroos, Antti Soini and Tuuli Kanerva from AS LL TK

"The younger generation often win because they think about things differently"

1

2

3

5

4

BACK TO THE FUTURE

Our modern cities have ever-evolving needs. But sometimes putting a new spin on an old idea might just fit the bill, whether the aim is to tackle climate change or simply entertain. **ILLUSTRATOR** *Ben Bueno*

I. ——— **Make it all white** *by Kimberly Bradley* ——— As global temperatures rise, painting rooftops white could help to cool our increasingly sweltering urban environments. ———

I recently had a phase of buying old furniture and then, armed with sandpaper, primer, brush and enamel, painting it all matte white. It was an attempt at minimalism, a reaction to the first five years of motherhood, which were filled with primary-coloured plastic and a lot of dirt. White, for me, was peace, visual clarity and maybe control, while across cultures and eras white has long symbolised holiness, purity, innocence, cleanliness and coolness.

In a less abstract sense, white reflects more light than darker colours, keeping surfaces cooler and hindering heat absorption. Zooming out from a burned-out mother's private apartment and given the urgency of climate change, why not paint entire cities white – or at least the rooftops?

With 50 to 65 per cent of their surfaces in dark-hued materials such as tar and asphalt – which do not reflect light, but rather capture heat and radiate it back into the atmosphere – cities get much warmer than the surrounding natural landscape. The temperature difference can reach up to 9C. "This is called urban heat load," says Dutch architect Ben van Berkel. Cities become "urban heat islands" in climate-control parlance and, on top of the discomfort of living in an oven (or paying too much for air-con), the dark surfaces can be significantly hotter than the surrounding air. Climate researchers and city-planners alike have been trying to devise multiple ways to reduce the load as cities grow – and green rooftops are perhaps the best-known example.

Another of their temperature-reduction initiatives is to simply paint rooftops (and, where possible, building façades or even roads) white. It's not a new idea: think of the gleaming white cuboid houses on the slopes of arid Greek islands, or the mostly light-coloured rooftops and façades in historically hot cities such as Athens, Jerusalem, Beirut and Bangkok. The rest of the world, as it heats up, is catching on. In the past decade nearly 950,000 sq m of New York's rooftops have been painted white through the CoolRoofs programme, which in part activates underemployed people and offers incentives to non-profits and landlords. Los Angeles is painting some of its asphalt streets white. Starting in 2015, Paris mandated rooftop environmental measures (either green roofs or white ones) and various Italian cities are running trials with white roofs.

Beyond conventional white paint, new coatings for super-cool rooftops and surfaces are also emerging. In collaboration with Swiss paint company Monopol Colors, Ben van Berkel's Amsterdam-based UNStudio developed The Coolest White, a paint that's ultra-durable; it launched in early 2019. Made of hi-tech polymers and lasting up to 30 years, it's engineered to really reflect sunlight. Darker materials absorb up to 95 per cent of the sun's rays and release them back into the atmosphere; normal white paint reduces this to 25 per cent. The Coolest White paint brings this value down to just 12 per cent. This hugely reduces the need for coolants and maybe even saves lives: the most dangerous factor in recent heatwaves has been nighttime overheating. Buildings don't cool down enough overnight for weaker or older people to recover from the physical stress of trying to beat the heat during the day.

The Coolest White can even be applied to steel, fibreglass and aluminium; the first applications will soon be underway. "We are doing a major master plan in India, a tech campus in Bangalore, where many buildings will have this coating," says Van Berkel, adding that The

Coolest White appears whiter or shinier depending on the angle it's seen from.

Architect Martin Haas of Haas Cook Zemmrich Studio 2050 in Stuttgart – a member of the German Sustainable Building Council – also sees white surfaces as a step in the right direction. "In terms of climate change, it's metaphorically five minutes to midnight, after all," he says. "And we need to do all we can."

He's still convinced that green rooftops remain the best option if they're possible. "Whenever you have a flat surface, it's better to not seal it. Stay in contact with Earth: make a green roof. It not only reflects, but also captures CO_2 and works as a storm water-management feature," he says. But if you have to seal a roof "then do it in a bright whitish colour", he adds. Van Berkel also says that his office, as well as Monopol Colors, is starting to think about other "coolest" colours, like The Coolest Green.

Haas recognises the need for greenery and light colours to creep back into city life in order to not only curb heat issues but to help people slowly reconnect with nature and, metaphorically, lighten up. As for me, I imagine future cities that have streets and façades of pure white (like too much of my furniture) or light green, baby blue or powdery pastels; some of them with greenery spilling down, others with farms on their rooftops. It sounds divine: quirky like the pictures in my daughter's old Dr Seuss books; a lot more soothing and certainly cooler than our sooty, dirty, hot roads and rooftops. Van Berkel remembers reading something that Andy Warhol said: "Wouldn't it be great if all the streets were made in carpet?" In white, please. — (M)

2. —— **Arcade games** *by Matthew Ponsford* —— Largely abandoned in the 20th century, shopping arcades are back with the promise of an enticing consumer experience. ——

Walking through Paris's Passage de l'Opéra at the start of the 20th century, the French surrealist writer Louis Aragon hallucinated that the shopping arcade was bathed in submarine green light, as if the whole structure was deep underwater. A skinny mermaid – naked "down to a very low waistline", with a tail of steel or rose petals – swam between walking canes in a shop window.

They tended to get like that, the surrealists. But Aragon points, too, to the lost spectacle of the shopping arcade. In the 19th and early 20th centuries, these arcades revealed an intoxicating collision of commerce, debate, round-the-clock eating and drinking, dance and play, which created a sensation among Parisian flâneurs and the booming urban bourgeoisie.

With no zoning regulations and little policing, arcades across Europe hosted brothels, bedsits, public baths, art galleries, theatres, hairdressers, cafés and shops selling books, stationery, coins and spices.

Passage de l'Opéra, which captivated both Aragon and the cultural theorist Walter

The arcade conspicuously evokes the golden age of Paris passages, carving a new route through a convent, a garage and an odd 1930s building by architect Henri Sauvage

Benjamin, was the first internationally acclaimed 24-hour destination. Through the day it acted as an illicit stock exchange (the so-called La Petite Bourse), then an all-night eating spot, art gallery, dancing destination and an after-party location for post-opera masked drinking. Structurally it was never more than a shopping street with a roof of iron and glass, lit up during the night with gas lamps. But it was the most important architectural form of the 19th century, said Benjamin: the architecture that birthed consumer society.

No retail location today fires such hot and confused passions. Least of all arcades, which often exhibitions and Instagram-bait wrapped around a consumerist conceptual "experience".

Arguably the best-known surviving arcade was an early standard-bearer for such reinvention. Galleria Vittorio Emanuele II, a glass-domed behemoth in Milan, was restored in 2015 by an unprecedented collaboration between Prada and Versace. The arcade, owned by the Commune of Milan, had hosted playful placemaking as early as 2003 when artists Elmgreen & Dragset's "Short Cut" installed a white Fiat Uno hatchback and caravan trailer, crashing through the decorative mosaic floor.

pay €1m a year to rent a shop with a single window in the arcade.

New arcades have followed. Beaupassage Paris, which opened in 2018, is a wellness-branded development of dining spots from celebrity chefs who cumulatively claim 17 Michelin stars. The arcade conspicuously evokes the golden age of Paris passages, carving a new route through a 17th-century convent, a garage from the 1960s and an odd 1930s building by architect Henri Sauvage.

Beaupassage inches closer to the round-the-clock destination that Paris once boasted with Passage de l'Opéra. It has become known as a world-class food court and somewhere to share a bottle of natural wine, amid installation art and a mini forest. But still, it is hardly Aragon's "ghostly landscape of damnable pleasures".

Excitement arrives, instead, in less orderly places. Two strangely

represent the stuffiest, most sterile streets of uniform luxury. It's time to imagine a way back.

The 20th century saw hundreds of arcades abandoned for department stores in London, Milan and Paris – including Passage de l'Opéra – or else preserved as museum-like curios. But early in the 21st century the raucous arcade makes business sense again, as shop-floor sales volumes become secondary to

Since reopening, the Renaissance Revival giant has doubled down. Fashion runways, including Prada Resort in 2018, have come to the raised Osservatorio level; new hotels have opened up in the wings; Milan Design Week commissions have arrived in the thoroughfare; and open-air cinema screenings have been hosted on the roof. For the city, the restoration has paid off. In 2018, Saint Laurent offered to

shaped developments have recently incubated gentrification-threatened communities: Sewoon Sangga, a repurposed Brutalist mega-complex in Seoul, and Peckham Palms, a hangar-like hub for south London hairdressers, cafés, and beauty salons evicted by a nearby regeneration project. These are buzzy buildings, full of surprises, where longstanding retailers and entrepreneurs are provided affordable units.

In Thailand, architect Alice Dietsch describes AL_A's 72 Courtyard as "space to breathe" amid Bangkok's hectic main drag, Thong Lo. The client, a nightclub manager, allowed the firm to leave space for a garden at the centre of the development to surprise and delight visitors – even if it this meant giving up rental income that could have come with in-filling that space with shops.

Both 72 Courtyard and its grass-roofed rival The Commons (across the street) consciously plumbed history, from arcades to Bangkok's own "community malls": open-air mini-shopping centres that are centred on green space. The aim was to provide an equivalent to the European squares in a city that lacks parks.

Dietsch explains that her client was "a guy with a really good sense of what people need to have a good time". Built around his nightclub, the development was innately 24-hour and inextricably linked to the heaving street of bars outside.

European and Asian arcade redevelopments often put the over-riding emphasis on strict "curation" of visitors' experiences. Thong Lo loosens such programming, in a return to some basic principles of the arcade. "The architecture is in the background. It's much more about the raw spaces and that's where interactions between people are made possible," says Dietsch.

There's open potential for city centres to go beyond this, as the business of trading goods vacates. But some space for excitement, darkness and invention must be carved out before they can become – to quote the patron saint of arcades one last time – "the true sanctuaries of a cult of the ephemeral". — (M)

3. —— **Room to grow** *by Louise Wright and Mauro Baracco, Baracco+Wright Architects* —— Plants like to live in the ground. What if we went back to basics and let them stay there? ——

We need to put a plant in a pot because we have displaced it from its home in the ground. In a rather Victorian manner we keep it contained for our own pleasure; it's wonderful to live among plants.

Keeping a plant alive in a container is a difficult task. Just ask the gardeners abseiling down the façade of Italian architect Stefano Boeri's impressive Bosco Verticale in Milan. While you're at it, why not glance over to the ivy-covered building next door, thriving with its roots in the soil, independent of human care.

At the Venice Architecture Biennale 2018 our practice, along with Linda Tegg, exposed the difficulty of replicating conditions in the Australian Pavilion: thousands of plants in pots grew under artificial lights. This displacement considered what's removed when we clear land. The plants in pots had to be cared for constantly, revealing how difficult it is to replace something once it's removed. Climate change played out inside the gallery, where temperature and humidity controls isolated the Australian plants from Venice's humidity.

Reflecting on how hard it is to keep a potted plant alive might guide us in a less artificial approach to how we bring plants back to places where they have been removed through urbanisation. What if we just put plants in the ground where they can communicate with each other and share water and nutrients through their mycorrhizal networks?

Are we ready to allow plants to live on their own terms? "Weeds", lichen and moss spontaneously grow in our cities. Urban environments are capable of remarkable diversity. If one can't empathise with the contained plant then the growing body of evidence of the benefits of vegetation in urban development is compelling. They include an increase in property values, crime reduction, human health, urban island heat effects, storm-water management and mitigation of climate change events. Architecture and urban design simply need to make more space for plants to have their roots in the ground. — (M)

A guide for freeing plants:

1. Set the plant free by putting it in the ground.
2. Try to keep the soil of the area, rather than adding any.
3. Try to make a space for multiple plants: they like to grow together.
4. Let sun, rain and oxygen in.

SUBSCRIBE

Subscribe to MONOCLE today to get a global perspective and fresh IDEAS direct to your door. One-year subscribers receive INVITES to events around the world and a limited-edition TOTE.

'I can confidently forecast that I'll be taking out a subscription'

ONE-YEAR PLUS
—
10 × MONOCLE, 3 × specials (including *The Drinking & Dining Directory*) + a tote bag.

ONE-YEAR PREMIUM
—
10 × MONOCLE, 3 × specials (including *The Drinking & Dining Directory*) + a Porter bag.

READY TO SUBSCRIBE?
—
Sign up today and "opt in" to receive the latest issue to hit the newsstand.

EXCLUSIVE DISCOUNT
—
Subscribers get 10 per cent off at all Monocle Shops – and online at *monocle.com/shop*.

SIGN UP NOW: MONOCLE.COM/FC20

DIFFERENT CLASS

Annabelle Chapman REPORTING FROM *Switzerland:* Recognising the impact that a school's design can have on a child's education, Swiss architects are leading the field in creating more accommodating institutions. We visit three that make the grade. PHOTOGRAPHER *Yves Bachmann*

"The school's approach is that kids can learn in any space; you don't have to build fences all over the place"

For many, memories of school involve drab corridors, cold classrooms and desks that had seen better days. Now, however, there's a growing awareness that it's not just how children learn that matters but *where* they learn. The surrounding shapes, colours and textures can help pupils to feel at ease or inspire them to be creative. Moreover, involving them in a school's design can become part of the learning process.

When you enter the primary school in Zofingen, roughly an hour's drive from Zürich, you notice the step-like sculptures in the hall. In bold shades of blue, pink, green and yellow, they contrast with the modern concrete-and-oak interior. "The idea is to connect the static building with its moving inhabitants in a playful way," says Zürich-based designer Sebastian Marbacher, perched on one of the sculptures. The young designer won a competition to provide an installation for the new school as part of the Kunst am Bau programme, which allocates funds for art in public buildings.

It resulted in six coated-foam objects (each of them big enough to be moveable only by adults) inside the school, while outside are 11 static works made with coloured concrete and gravel. "What I did not expect is that they are more of an obstacle to jump over than to sit on," says Marbacher. As we watch, two small boys wearing rucksacks throw themselves onto some yellow steps. Minutes later a girl clambers over a blue structure on her way outside.

According to the designer, the objects encourage pupils to mingle and appropriate their new school building. "It can kill a lot of ideas if the rules are too strict," he says, in relation to the architecture of a school. "This school's approach is that kids can learn in any space; you don't have to build fences all over the place."

In Basel the spatial-design studio ZMIK developed its "learning landscapes" at the St Johann Primary School, an imposing building finished in 1880. During recent

1

2

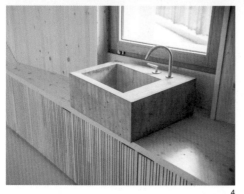

lockers for the older students – feature in the final design. Mohr and his colleagues chose materials with a range of textures: painted timber, polished oak, linoleum, upholstered surfaces and grass-like carpeting.

"Pedagogical concepts are changing and influencing projects such as this," says Mohr as we pass a group of pupils working at a table attached to the windowsill (part of the installation). "This space contrasts with the classroom, with its chairs and desks. It is more fluid – children can figure out how to use it themselves." An echo of the modern workplace? "If you look at work today it's very similar. You want different spaces and can be working even if it looks like you're hanging around."

The installations have fostered a sense of responsibility: the school's cleaning service doesn't include them, so pupils have been vacuuming them themselves. "This is a pioneer landscape," says Mohr, who hopes the project's success will encourage similar investments at other primary schools.

At the Rudolf Steiner School in Geneva, a private school based on the philosophy of the Austrian educator, which pupils can

Previous page: Zofingen primary school entrance hall

This spread:
1. Modern lighting, Zofingen
2. ZMIK's 'learning landscapes', Basel
3. Larch-wood upper floor in Geneva
4. Classroom sink, Geneva
5. School cafeteria, Geneva

renovations, the educational authorities agreed on a budget for built-in furniture on the condition that the pupils were involved in the design process. The competition was won by ZMIK which created a combined cloakroom and learning space for the school's corridors.

"The main idea was to create extra space to learn in or, rather, to learn in a different way," says Mattias Mohr, a partner at ZMIK. "Our aim was to not just place furniture in the corridor but rather melt it with the building's historical architecture," he adds, noting the challenge posed by safety and fire regulations.

Displaying soft green tones, the installation resembles an abstract landscape, with slides, caves and perches for the younger children and group seating for the older ones. Some of the pupils' ideas – such as

1.
Sebastian
Marbacher's
sculptures in
the entrance
hall, Zofingen
2.
View from
the top floor,
Geneva
3.
Window detail
in Zofingen

4.
School library,
Zofingen
5.
Classroom in
Geneva

2 3

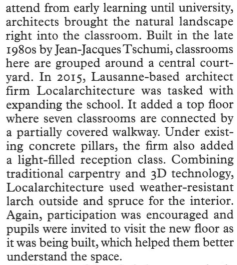

4

attend from early learning until university, architects brought the natural landscape right into the classroom. Built in the late 1980s by Jean-Jacques Tschumi, classrooms here are grouped around a central courtyard. In 2015, Lausanne-based architect firm Localarchitecture was tasked with expanding the school. It added a top floor where seven classrooms are connected by a partially covered walkway. Under existing concrete pillars, the firm also added a light-filled reception class. Combining traditional carpentry and 3D technology, Localarchitecture used weather-resistant larch outside and spruce for the interior. Again, participation was encouraged and pupils were invited to visit the new floor as it was being built, which helped them better understand the space.

"It's part of the whole but a completely different world, connected with the sky," says architect and Localarchitecture partner Antoine Robert-Grandpierre as we reach the top floor, where the teenage pupils have their classes. "You feel like you're in a treehouse." Whereas the classrooms on the lower floors feel cocooned, the top floor offers the older pupils views of the Jura Mountains to the north and the Salève range to the south. Thanks to their skylights, pale wooden walls and simple desks and chairs from Vitra, the classrooms provide a serene space for learning. "When you enter the classroom, the atmosphere should be totally different from outside – it should be calm and light," says Robert-Grandpierre.

These examples show that Switzerland is ahead of the curve when it comes to viewing school design as an investment in the next generation. Firstly, bright colours, engaging textures and flexible spaces support playfulness and creativity, especially among young children. Secondly, warm natural materials help pupils and teachers feel calm and focused in class, while making the space feel less like a prison.

Finally, involving children in the design process encourages their sense of pride and ownership in their surroundings. Even without generous Swiss budgets, these are principles that schools around the world can apply, whether that means perking up their existing spaces or bringing in bright architects, such as this Swiss bunch, for the betterment of education. — (M)

5

TALKING THREADS

Jamie Waters REPORTING ON *fashion:* It's an industry where there's always plenty to talk about. We brought together a fashion designer, a PR guru and a menswear buyer to discuss the direction it's heading in – and the challenges it faces. PHOTOGRAPHER *Ben Quinton*

Sustainability, runway shows, the fate of department stores and our shifting shopping habits are perennial hot topics in the fashion industry. That's why we gathered three experts in our radio studio at Midori House to gaze into fashion's crystal ball and hammer out the big issues.

Our guests have contrasting backgrounds. Paula Gerbase, a Brazil-born, London-based fashion designer, was behind cult unisex label 1205, which closed in 2016; she also recently launched Gerbase, a brand offering women's bespoke tailoring, fine jewellery and knitwear. In addition she's the artistic director of bootmaker John Lobb.

Representing the buyers is Dean Cook. He previously worked in sales for Prada, Jil Sander and Versace and is now the head of menswear buying at Browns, the London retail institution that turns 50 next year and is opening a new flagship in Mayfair.

Adam Shapiro is our PR guru. The American was previously at Burberry and KCD, and is the founder of L52 Communications, a London agency whose clients include The Row, Bally and Dutch up-and-comer Wandler. — (M)

all the fireworks. It's funny because I was based in London but we were Japan-centric. But when you start to sell to the West, other pressures come along. The way we judge success as an industry can be quite limiting: if you're a brand and you don't aspire to do shows there's something wrong with you.

What convinced you to do them then?
PG: We got sponsorship from the BFC [British Fashion Council], specifically to do a show. It works for lots of brands

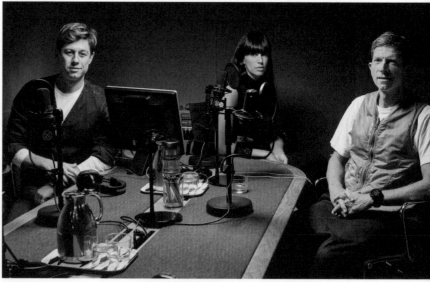

1

There has been a lot of discussion surrounding whether the traditional catwalk model will last. Paula, you did runway shows with 1205 – what do you think?
PAULA GERBASE: I started 1205 with a collection of 12 unisex, genderless pieces that got picked up in Japan and grew from there. When I started we didn't do runway shows – I was very much against them. I just wanted to create clothing and my goal wasn't to see it on *vogue.com*; I wanted to see it worn on the street. The Japanese are good at picking up brands without needing

1.
Our roundtable (from left): Adam Shapiro, Paula Gerbase and Dean Cook

but I think it also puts pressure on young businesses who could probably be using that money to, I don't know, run their businesses. Because ultimately your goal is to have longevity. That said, the shows took us from being an underground brand to big retailers knocking on our door. All the department stores are suddenly interested in what you're doing because you're in this format that they understand. But I think it also draws a certain kind of customer that you don't necessarily share values with.

Adam, you're in the business of building brand awareness. Is a runway show still the best way to do that?

ADAM SHAPIRO: It's not a one-size-fits-all mentality anymore. For big brands, shows are critical. Because on top of the budget to do a special show they bring all their social-media might, all their press stuff, all their VIP-dressing-influencer stuff. There are so many other elements of their communications strategy, which means that the show is one of the big peaks for them – but then it lives on for the rest of the season. Think about a really big recent show: the Versace womenswear show.

When Jennifer Lopez closed the spring/summer 2020 show in a replica of the famous Versace gown she wore to the Grammys in 2000…

AS: Not only are you getting huge attention at the time of the show, because of J-Lo, but you also have a conversation that builds for the rest of the season. But that is a mega-brand approach; they can afford to do something like that and they need to be seen, compared to their peers, as behaving in that sort of way. For a small or mid-level brand a show is a very different proposition. It depends on how much budget you have allocated, your creative process and your production timelines. All these things become important when you're smaller because you have to allocate your dollars so that you get the most bang for your buck.

PG: But it's not just about how you allocate your marketing budgets: it also comes down to values and what you want to say as a brand. The Versace example is interesting because I actually have no idea what that collection looked like. All I know is that J-Lo walked the finale and people were going crazy about it. But maybe it's OK [that I don't know about the collection] because it is getting attention to that brand at that moment.

> "It's not a one-size-fits all mentality any more. For big brands shows are critical"

> "A runway brand is growing its business through a more niche audience at the beginning"

Does the Versace example just highlight the fact that the goal of a fashion show now is to create a big Instagram moment?

DEAN COOK: Well, if J-Lo didn't walk that catwalk, we wouldn't be talking about Versace, would we? The razzmatazz has lifted the brand to another level.

AS: I do think there are younger designers for whom the show is genuinely a creative expression. And they use it as an opportunity to not only showcase the clothing but also build a universe.

DC: Do most young brands want to get to the runway?

AS: Many young brands would consider themselves a "runway brand" so they want to put on a show. But I work with other brands that have zero interest in a runway show.

PG: But does that make them lesser than the runway brands?

AS: Not at all – it means they have a different approach to growing their business. A runway brand is growing its business through a much more niche fashion audience at the beginning, hoping to build coolness and exclusivity and have that filter out from there. Another brand might want a presentation, great digital content and a kick-ass social-media strategy. And maybe they have a stronger direct-to-consumer model versus a wholesale model. But I think the cleverer brands have something they're working towards and use a runway show – or another format – as a means to get there.

PG: I think, as an industry, creativity and high-end means runway. And when we talk about not doing runway we talk about straight-to-consumer and more commercial strategies. I'm interested in expressing something that's creative – but not a runway show. I'm interested in whether that's actually more creative than always falling back on a runway show as the only form of presentation for fashion as a medium.

AS: I think there could be lots of interesting ways to present a collection that aren't runway but ultimately there needs to be a commercial component to what you're doing. Because if you're going to survive and sell something you have to somehow disseminate the visuals of what you've created to a wider audience. So you need to think how can people buy it, where they buy it and what it looks like.

Paula, are you thinking of a format that could replace a runway show?
PG: I think about that all the time. I'm not saying I will never do a show but I'm asking, "Are there more interesting alternatives?" Maybe they are straight to consumer; maybe they are a press presentation that isn't just people standing around. I don't have the answer. But there must be ways that go beyond categorising "high-end" collections as being shown on runways, and "commercial" straight-to-consumer collections as being shown digitally. Because those boundaries are blurred. You know, the Versace moment was a digital moment…

AS: And let's not discount the talent involved [with Versace]. I mean, from J-Lo's perspective, she has a new movie to promote [*Hustlers*]. And, in the wake of its acquisition by Michael Kors, Versace would want to emphasise that the brand hasn't changed – it's still the Versace we know and love. So it links together very cleverly from both sides. It's a masterclass in collaboration.

PG: What does that have to do with fashion though?

> "The industry has changed so much. The McQueen shows were pure creativity"

AS: It has to do with commerce and awareness – I'm not sure it has much to do with creativity, necessarily.

PG: That's what I find interesting. We talk about runways as being these moments of pure, unadulterated creativity but the show that we're talking about from last season was a beautifully executed marketing exercise.

AS: The industry has changed so much. I mean, we can remember the McQueen shows, which were pure expressions of creativity. But it's a very different world now because back then they didn't have to sing digitally: they only had to engage the audience that was in the room and make them feel like they were part of something special. Now it has to translate digitally to a global audience too. The runway show has to do something different for today's brands than when it could be a purely creative play.

Dean, as a buyer, how much attention do you pay to the runway shows?
DC: They're super important for me because it's what the consumer sees. A runway show is in all the magazines, on social media – everyone's talking about it. Yes, I agree with Paula that it has become a bit of a circus but runways also give brands a chance to show what they're all about. I think the runways are great.

PG: Another reason I couldn't really justify runway shows in the end was the sustainability question. I have had arguments with friends who are producers. They've said, "Oh, but the benches are rented." And I've said, "Yes but I know you binned that carpet." Everyone wants beautiful printed invitations but then they throw them on the floor after the show. There are printed seating cards. There's, I don't know, icebergs being flown in. There's such a huge amount of waste.

DC: I think we're going to see a lot of change there though. Sustainability is the first thing that many brands are talking about now.

PG: I was quite frustrated last season because there was so much talk from brands about the importance of the environment. Meanwhile, look at the amount that is being produced – the fabric wastage, the shipping, the shows. It's not enough to say it: the values need to be followed through.

DC: We have a whole sustainability department in the Farfetch office [Browns is owned by Farfetch] that's looking at how sustainable brands are. If you're a brand it's about showing that you're trying these things.

PG: But *truly* trying, rather than just talking about it.

AS: There's no chance any brand can reach 100 per cent sustainability so it's about doing the absolute best you can – within

"It's not enough to say it. Values need to be followed through"

the means of your survival. Because it's pointless to make all these moves if the brand is not going to stick around; sadly there has to be an element of the conversation that allows brands to be profitable.

Sustainability can feel like a buzzword.
AS: From a PR perspective it's really cringey when you're championing sustainability at the top of your press release. It needs to be a major pillar that underpins your business. But if it's at the top of a press release it makes you question what the brand is up to.

It makes it seem like the selling point.
AS: And it shouldn't be. It should be such a natural part of your day-to-day business that it doesn't supersede anything else. But consumers can just rely on the fact that you're doing the best you can with your supply chain. That's the goal: for sustainability not to be such a unique thing that it sets a brand apart.

PG: I had an interesting online shopping experience recently. I spend a lot of time outside and there's one outerwear brand at the forefront of talking about the environment: Patagonia. Their things are truly great quality. But I ordered a garment from their website and it arrived at my house in two layers of plastic. As a customer who felt like I shared the brand's values, I found that shocking. That's when I think about true values versus a marketing strategy to target millennial audiences.

There's also this tension because the fashion industry is premised on selling lots of things, which is at odds with not creating waste.
AS: You have people saying, "OK, buy one fabulous thing that you're going to wear forever." That's a slightly classist statement because there are people who can't afford

that one thing that will last forever. You have to engage the fast-fashion brands as well in terms of cleaning up their practices.

DC: But the fashion thing is not to have it last a lifetime. We're doing a sneaker launch and then next week we're telling you to buy another pair. We're doing four drops a week. We're telling you to buy as much as possible. It's like anything: you want, you want, you want – you get. And then you get bored and you want something else.

PG: I actually don't think "fast fashion" is a big ugly phrase. There's space for all types of fashion but it's about doing it with integrity. You can look at the way you manufacture things whether you're at luxury or high-street level.

DC: The good thing is everyone is taking notice. I feel it's come upon us very quickly. For me this is the biggest trend. Although I've noticed there are much more women's than menswear brands that are engaging with sustainability.

"There's space for all types of fashion but it's about doing it with integrity"

PG: My worry is that it is a trend. That next season it will be something else.

DC: I don't think so. It must stay on our radar.

There's lots of chat now about Barneys and the future of department stores. Is this a concern?
DC: I don't think you can put all department stores into the same category. Just look at Selfridges: it's a hugely successful business.

AS: The American department stores are a specific thing unto themselves. There's definitely some reckoning going on there. Here in London the department-store networks aren't as large so they've managed to really focus on each store.

DC: If you think about our three biggest department stores [Selfridges, Harrods and Liberty], they're so different from one another.

Whereas one of the criticisms levelled at Barneys was that it lost a point of view and became too generic.
AS: Totally. It didn't feel like the unique place where you would go to find brands that you couldn't find anywhere else. As an American transplant living in London, I think that the London department stores do a very good job of getting customers in and keeping them for a long time. At department stores in the States there's less to keep you interested, by and large. Here you can spend the whole day in Selfridges, just like that.

Dean, what does a fashion shop need to do today to thrive?
DC: We sit around the table every week talking about this. For me the most important thing is product. Because why are you going to a boutique? You're not going because it's got a great staircase or

a fantastic garden. You're going to look at product – at things that are different from what you can get elsewhere. That other stuff is around creating an experience.

Everyone is now saying that shops need to create an 'experience'. How important do you think that actually is and how do you deliver it?
DC: Every three to four weeks at Browns East [Browns' Shoreditch outpost] we change the store, from the entrance to the pop-up area to the full brand mix. And every three months the café changes.

PG: It sounds exhausting.

DC: It is but it means that every time you go in you'll see something different. We have pop-up areas with exclusive launches, capsule collections and art installations. We have a running club that goes from the store, plus music and parties. It's about engaging the community as well.

AS: It's clever the way Browns is an international name but you also localise the store. Plenty of stores rely on tourists and I think that's to their detriment. You need to have a natural relationship with your immediate surroundings – to have locals coming in to shop.

Do you worry that online shopping will kill physical retail?
PG: Online is the norm now. But online is for picking your uniform: I'll get socks and another six T-shirts. I don't need to have an experience buying sports socks. When you go into a store you want to feel something, whether it's about having a relationship with the people there or touching the product. Some products, like ski boots or bespoke shoes, are hard to buy online – you have to try them. These are based on a long-lasting relationship between artisan and customer. I don't think the human side of those relationships

> **"Online is for picking your uniform. I don't need an experience buying sports socks"**

will ever go away; I think we're craving them more. Also, if I want to discover, I don't know, a new brand from Argentina, maybe I check their Instagram and see that they have a pop-up at Browns. And then there's a way I can interact with them in a very direct and human way, which is quite modern really. Most people think the digital sphere has distanced people but actually, in some ways, it's given us the opportunity – as brands – to be closer to a customer. That's a great thing. Communication has become easier and

we're more accessible to one another. I find it interesting when a customer just sends me a DM [direct message on Instagram]. That direct feedback is really heartwarming. I think that human connection hasn't been lost – it's actually been highlighted.

Tune in:
This conversation was also recorded for *On Design*, MONOCLE's design-themed radio show. Tune in at *monocle.com/radio/shows* – or listen via iTunes, Spotify or wherever you get your podcasts.

TAKING STOCK

Hamish Anderson REPORTING FROM *New York:* E-commerce has had a transformative effect on city centres but now the booming demand for warehouses to speed-up last-mile deliveries is set to bring another round of dramatic change to our urban landscape. ILLUSTRATOR *Alberto Casagrande*

New York doesn't feel like the future. The subway is decaying and filthy; there are human-sized piles of rubbish on pavements; and fashion and music trends increasingly come from elsewhere. But activities at two Brooklyn warehouses – one under construction, the other a century old – show that the city is at the forefront of one key debate: the competing visions for our urban future.

The most visible impact of e-commerce on cities has been the decline of bricks-and-mortar shops. And this looks set to continue: according to Swiss investment bank UBS, 75,000 stores will close in the US over the next seven years. But there's another way that e-commerce is reshaping cities: warehouses.

Online shopping is fuelling a warehouse real-estate boom. According to the Deloitte Center for Financial Services, demand for distribution centres and other types of industrial real estate increased by 81 million sq m between 2014 and 2018; similar growth is projected over the next four years. Amazon now occupies about 23 million sq m of space globally, most of it warehouses; that's equivalent to 5,000 football pitches. Net-a-Porter has distribution centres on four continents; Ali Baba is building multiple logistics networks at Hong Kong International Airport to meet demand from across China; and Blackstone Group has bought a network of US warehouses from Singapore-based GLP for $18.7bn (€16.6bn) in what is being called the largest ever private real-estate transaction.

Warehouses and "third-party logistics centres" (known in the trade as 3PLS) are being built from Slovakia to Singapore. So far they're mostly in hinterlands or near transit hubs on the outskirts of cities. But their impact on urban centres might change with the rise of next-day delivery and increased demand for so-called last-mile services. "Without a doubt, the take-up of space within city limits will increase to meet last-mile demand," says Sally Duggleby,

a senior consultant at property manager Savills, who was previously head of property for Amazon in the UK and Ireland. Customers in major cities increasingly expect items bought online to be delivered a few hours later. For that to happen, those items must be stored nearby – and that brings us to Brooklyn.

Sunset Industrial Park is a handful of shabby squat buildings overlooked by the Brooklyn-Queens expressway. To the untrained eye it doesn't seem likely to be worth hundreds of millions of dollars. But

its location – within an hour's drive of 13 million consumers in Manhattan, Brooklyn and beyond – means that it could be of tremendous value to an e-commerce company. That's why developers Dov Hertz and Bridge Development Partners bought the 7.3-hectare site in 2019 for $255m (€226m). After construction, which starts in 2020, the site will have a 12-storey warehouse that spans the equivalent of 17 football pitches, making it the largest multi-storey warehouse in the US. But what's most notable is that it's within a few minutes' walk of increasingly popular residential neighbourhoods.

As creative types have been pushed deeper into Brooklyn – into areas such as

Kids are being taught to do a job that their future employers are trying hard to eradicate

Gowanus and Sunset Park – due to rising rents, the idea of what constitutes the city's "outskirts" is changing. In Gowanus, high-end restaurants and nightclubs now share space with autobody shops in a manner that resembles 1990s Manhattan. Whether a giant warehouse will enhance the area is debatable but these neighbourhoods' longtime residents might see one as a boon for local employment.

Yet, given the rise in automation, it's uncertain how many jobs a warehouse can create and how dependable they

will be. In California's Central Valley at least one school has started offering classes on how to be "pickers"; a warehouse job (that robots can't do) involving selecting items for shipment. But is that the best way to prepare students for the future? Companies that rely on warehouses are trying their best to make human workers obsolete. Amazon, for instance, is funding an annual competition to design a robot that can take over the role of a picker.

An alternative vision for warehouses exists five minutes up the road at Industry City, a vast complex mainly built at the start of the 20th century. When developers took over in 2013 their chief goal

"Without a doubt, the take-up of space within city limits will increase to meet last-mile demand"

was to move Industry City away from warehousing towards high employment uses. It now has more than 500 tenants – many of them start-ups – running the gamut from graphic designers and cupcake-makers to manufacturers, film-industry suppliers and architects. The atmosphere is lively and the site currently has 7,500 jobs. But are any of them going to long-term residents? "We have an on-site jobs and entrepreneurship centre, run by a non-profit that has been in the neighbourhood for decades, geared towards local communities," says a representative.

Industry City isn't all about altruism. While the firm is aware that "the need for new last-mile facilities has dramatically increased over the past few years", it is sticking to its existing model rather than taking the complex back to its warehousing roots. It wants the sort of money and security that having an e-commerce company as a tenant would bring but intends to get that by attracting office, retail and hotels instead. Industry City is bustling but, says the representative, if you change it to warehousing, "There's no ecosystem; nothing's happening."

But in the future, how many landlords will take this route? Demand usually wins out in the property game. So while urban residents probably won't want a warehouse as a neighbour, they might need to get used to it. Globally, e-commerce growth is expected to remain between 14 and 19 per cent annually for the next few years, which means that many more goods will have to be stored near customers. Market research firm Market Study Report LLC says that the value of the global market for last-mile delivery will grow by more than 50 per cent in the next five years. The Sunset Industrial Park warehouse won't be the last of its kind. But while these facilities bring goods back into the heart of cities, they are unlikely to recreate the dynamism of high streets past. — (M)

New podcast from MONOCLE

'The Masters' introduces you to pioneers from the fields of design, art, fashion, music and more. Hear their philosophies, which have brought them to the very top of their profession.

Here are some of the inspirational innovators you'll meet. Find all the shows at monocle.com or wherever you get your podcasts.

Reed Krakoff Tiffany's chief artistic officer, a master of innovation, on stewarding a storied name.

Scott Campbell The world-renowned tattoo artist, and owner of legendary Saved Tattoo in Brooklyn, New York, explains why his craft doesn't end at the tip of a needle.

MONOCLE 24

The Masters

TIFFANY & CO.

David de Rothschild The explorer, adventurer and campaigner (*pictured*) on why he remains optimistic about a sustainable future for our planet.

Ronan Bouroullec Ronan and his brother Erwan run their eponymous design studio from Belleville in Paris. Find out what drives their pursuit of excellence.

Sam Bompas One half of Bompas & Parr reveals how the duo work to colonise people's imaginations.

LISTEN LIVE AT MONOCLE.COM OR SUBSCRIBE TO OUR PODCASTS; ALSO ON ITUNES, SPOTIFY AND ALL GOOD AUDIO PLATFORMS

WE'RE SOLD

With the right ingredients, physical shops can not only survive but thrive in today's climate. The retailers on these pages show what you can do with a little imagination, an eye for quality and a genuine desire to look after your customers.

1.
Beige
Habilleur
shopfront
in Paris
2.
Customer
Julien Milla
3.
Fox umbrellas

Beige Habilleur
Paris

"We're not into the fantasy of a guy from the 1930s wearing a complete tweed suit – that's too extravagant for today," says Basile Khadiry, co-owner of Beige Habilleur, Paris's standout contemporary menswear boutique. "We have tailoring but we also have sneakers – as long as they are well made."

Khadiry – who has previously worked for Louis Vuitton and Ami – and his business partner Jean-Baptiste Ménétrier started Beige Habilleur as an e-commerce business in 2015, before they opened the bricks-and-mortar location in 2018. It's in a former sushi shop on a bustling road in the city's 16th arrondissement. The bourgeois, family-friendly neighbourhood is undergoing a cultural boost thanks to influential residents such as artistic director Franck Durand, who opened Holiday café and its retail arm Holiday Boileau nearby and encouraged Khadiry to follow him. Durand worked on the art direction of Beige Habilleur alongside Paris-based architectural duo Lecoadic-Scotto. They outfitted the store with polished concrete flooring, pine cabinetry and a ceiling painted a David Hockney blue.

The modern, light-filled space feels right for this refreshing mix of menswear, which spans cool tailoring, sportswear and great knits. There's an exclusive selection of UK brands such as coats from Grenfell and Mackintosh, sought-after Japanese names such as Cohérence and denim brand Resolute, and timeless styles from German knitwear line Heimat and US sportswear brand Camber. There's also a concession store for Drake's, which occupies a small corner space. The offerings extend beyond clothes: titles from leading French magazine distributor Les Editions du Kiosque occupy one of the walls.

2

1.
Belts by
L'Aiglon
2.
Basile Khadiry
3.
Dapper
mannequins
4.
Bucket hat by
Lock and Co,
sweater by Inis
Meáin, jacket
by Grenfell

5.
Deck Shoes
by Doek
6.
Full look
by Drake's

Such in-store exclusives and personal touches, including a made-to-measure service for Justo Gimeno's famous Teba jackets and an alterations service with local denim aficionado Super Stitch, has seen the brand transition successfully from an e-commerce presence to a destination store. Plus the neighbourhood, says Khadiry, is assuredly on the up. "Now a lot of people are moving back from the east of the city to the west, where they were born and raised." Besides, he adds, shopping in the Marais just isn't what it used to be: "Real people aren't even living there anymore; it is just full of Airbnbs."

What stands out most is Khadiry's obsession with tracking down exceptionally made items with a unique sartorial history. They include the efforts of Irish shoemaker Padmore & Barnes, which

3

Basile Khadiry's top picks:

1.
Doek shoes: Japanese deck shoes made from kimono fabric.

2.
Teba jacket by Julio Gimeno: An iconic Spanish item that's a mix between an overshirt and a jacket.

3.
Camber mock neck: A true US workwear brand.

4

"In each category we find the best in terms of quality and design"

5

made the original Wallabee for Clarks, and French tie-maker Boivin, which made ties for historic Parisian shirt-maker Charvet. "In each category we find the best in terms of quality and design."

If there is something Khadiry can't find he'll probably just get it made in-house, as he has with a new line of shirts released under the Beige Habilleur brand. "We couldn't find the right old Oxford shirt, like Brooks Brother or J Press in the 1960s with the six buttons and no lining in the collar or cuffs," he says. The shirts are made in France in light, easy fabrics and Khadiry was fastidious about every element. "In the 1990s the logo was the message – now it's more about how it's made, why it's made that way and where it is made." — ALC
beigehabilleur.com

6

Lapo
Lisbon

Lisbon's booming tourist scene has seen the inevitable upswing in restaurant and shop openings aimed at cashing in on the influx of travellers. Yet how many more stores selling tinned seafood or fusion dining concepts does the Portuguese capital need? Husband-and-wife team António and Bruna Guerreiro decided to address the issue head on by opening Lapo, a new shop-meets-gallery-meets-restaurant geared towards residents and visitors eager for a bite, good conversation and a bit of culture. "Talking with friends, we noticed going out had become a dull experience, with everything geared towards moving people through the door and treating them as numbers," says António.

Opened this autumn in the Bica neighbourhood in central Lisbon, much of Lapo occupies a former bakery that has been tastefully converted into a shop; it sells clothing and accessories designed or commissioned by the couple and produced in Portugal. During renovation they uncovered a nook behind a stone arch and placed the cashier's desk there. An original marble wall was retained, while the remaining space was painted in a soothing shade of navy. Patrons browse a smart selection of T-shirts, tiles, ceramic sculptures and prints, many of which feature

1
"Culture is good for the soul. We've just reimagined it with retail and food"

2

I.
Patrons at the upstairs bar
2.
Entertainment includes comedy
3.
Ana Câmara, Lapo's artistic director
4.
Clothing in the Lapo shop
5.
Dressing-room door leading to restaurant

playful black-and-white designs by Bruna herself – the gifted illustrator from Brazil studied at Central St Martins in London.

The twist in this easygoing retail model is the hidden attraction behind the changing room, which in the evenings is opened to reveal a low-lit room for dining, drinking and taking in a show. The tasting menu is not overly complicated, with dishes including duck breast in a pear-and-orange sauce. The entertainment varies from night to night, be it a jazz trio, stand-up comedy or performance art, where audience participation is encouraged. "We wanted to inject the arts into the equation and get people to interact, linger and just have a good time," says António.

Upstairs the atmosphere is relaxed, with a café that serves tapas-style dishes and communal seating where patrons eat

at wooden tables once used by bakers to knead dough. In adjoining rooms you'll find a bar serving cocktails with names inspired by great thinkers (try the Carl Jung creation made with Lourinhã brandy, lemon juice, egg whites and Angostura bitters) and a relaxed lounge lined with books and vinyl where, on weekends, a resident DJ plays.

The owners are buoyed by the initial response, with locals and tuned-in holiday-makers eager to catch a show and browse Bruna's designs. A fun take on the "concept store" formula, Lapo inspires a convivial atmosphere and doesn't take itself too seriously. Adds António: "Culture is good for the soul. We've just reimagined it with retail and food." — IC
lapo.pt

3

4

What to buy:

1.
Illustrated T-shirts
with catchy phrases

2.
Simple black-and-white prints

3.
Paintings and photographs
by up-and-coming artists
are for sale upstairs

5

DSM's single-item focus – a new direction for retail?

The opening of Dover Street Parfums Market in Paris offers a glimpse of a different retail direction. Rather than offering a wide range of categories, this multibrand space – which the Dover Street Market (DSM) brand calls a "satellite store" – homes in on fragrances and beauty products.

Owners Rei Kawakubo and Adrian Joffe have found success over the past 15 years with their six multibrand, multi-product DSM shops in London, Tokyo, New York, LA, Singapore and Beijing. It's a an idea that has been copied by many but never bettered – and DSM remains at the forefront of fashion retail.

Dover Street Parfums Market focuses on one of the mothership's bestselling and more accessible categories. And because it is a smaller boutique than the six DSM outposts, rent and overheads are reduced. These lower risks mean the model has greater potential for growth beyond the world's shopping capitals.

The two-storey shop, just off the well-trodden paths of Le Marais, offers recognisable names alongside cult perfume brands and indie labels. Dover Street Parfums Market is the only place in Paris to discover Berlin botanical fragrance brand AER, low-fi natural beauty line Pure by Switzerland, and famed make-up artist Gucci Westman's own line, Westman Atelier. Bigger names, such as Byredo, Gucci and Thom Browne, have designed their own display units.

Looking ahead there's certainly room, says Joffe, to apply the single-product multibrand concept to other items, such as T-shirts, trainers and jewellery. "It's where we can really work on the incubation of young designers, [where] we can give that Dover Street energy," he says. It's a refreshing contrast to the ubiquitous concept store approach seen in retail today. Bring on the age of single-item shopping. — ALC

Von Maur
Davenport, Iowa

It's only November but in one section of the NorthPark Mall in Davenport, Iowa, Christmas has come early. The entrance to Von Maur – the original location of a department store chain with 35 shops, mostly in the Midwest – is graced by two large Christmas trees, with more visible inside, perched beneath garlands of pine needles hanging from the ceiling. The light is warm and inviting. There are two convincing replica fireplaces, plenty of elegant wood panelling and piano music wafting around, not from speakers but a Yamaha upright played by a woman with a pile of songbooks next to her.

As many US department stores go bankrupt, from the internationally renowned (Barneys) to the strictly regional (ever heard of Younkers?), Von Maur is not just surviving but thriving. It opened two new shops in 2019, with plans to open one or two more annually "for the next several years", according to director of advertising and e-marketing Jessica Stoltz. The company, whose spaces tend to anchor big shopping malls, has experienced "steady growth, which enables us to continue opening doors in the measured way that we do", adds Stoltz. The firm has been owned by the Von Maur family for 147 years; the family tends to avoid press (they declined to speak for this article) and don't share sales data about their company.

That family ownership is key to the company's success according to retail expert Nicole Reyhle, co-founder of the Independent Retailer Conference. "Because they are privately held they don't have the same pressure from investors that places like Sears have," she says, referring to another once-admired, now-bankrupt chain. "Von Maur's values and perspective on business are a little different to those of a publicly traded company. As stores have concentrated on online, many have lost focus on bricks and mortar – but Von Maur decided to continue to focus on what I'd call old-school customer service."

Staff at the Davenport store are attentive and helpful. When asked what they like about working at Von Maur, everyone mentions customer interaction first. Leona

1.
Von Maur
store in
Omaha,
Nebraska

Hedquist, who has been at Von Maur for 30 years and works in the men's department, says: "The Von Maur family are very good at hiring people who like people. If we cannot help a customer here we're going to send them to a place where they can help you. And Sofia here," she adds, gesturing to a colleague, "if you buy a dress shirt, she'll steam it for you. I keep a stash of candy for the men, because men do not like to shop on the whole." Many staff have been with Von Maur for decades and it is known to pay well compared to similar businesses.

Customers seem as happy as the staff. "They still do gift wrapping – a lot of stores don't," says shopper Kimberly Johnson. Von Maur also does free US shipping from its shops and there's no time limit on returns.

Von Maur seems highly attuned to its markets too. It has ample selections from

1

brands such as Kate Spade, Tory Burch and MZ Wallace, which are quite fashion forward in a city whose major employers are tractor brand John Deere and the US army.

No one would call Von Maur "directional" but the shop exudes a specific point of view in a way that department store chains tend not to. Goods reflect how locals shop: cashmere scarves and Chicago Bears hats are displayed near each other, since a man might need both. People wanting face creams will find a Kiehl's store, rather than a generic Clinique selection.

"Retail is not dying, it's simply evolving," says Reyhle. "Consumers are demanding stronger experiences." Which means some of Von Maur's traditional tendencies – old-school service and live music – are a strength in modern times. — HAN
vonmaur.com

"The Von Maur family are good at hiring people who like people"

STRIKE A POSE

Feeling confident? Good: 2020 is the year to be bold, put yourself out there and get noticed. And where better to start than with your wardrobe? These are the looks that will help you stand out from the crowd all year. PHOTOGRAPHER *Thomas Chéné*. WOMEN'S STYLIST *Daphné Hézard* MEN'S STYLIST *Shun Katakai*.

COAT by *Mackintosh*, GLASSES by *Lindberg*

THIS PAGE: JUMPER by *CristaSeya*, SHIRT and EARRINGS by *Celine*, TROUSERS by *Patou*,
BAG by *Hermès*

OPPOSITE: SHIRT by *Scye Basics*, JEANS by *Arket*

THIS PAGE: JACKET and TROUSERS by *Orazio Luciano*, SHIRT by *Tod's*, SHOES by *Church's*

OPPOSITE: SHIRT and TRAINERS by *Celine*, JEANS by *Crista Seya*, EARRINGS by *Patou*

JACKET by *Drake's*,
SWEATSHIRT by *Colmar*,
TROUSERS by *A Kind
of Guise*, SANDALS
by *Birkenstock*

ROLLNECK JUMPER, SKIRT and SHOES by *Chanel*, EARRINGS by *Celine*,
BANGLES by *Saint Laurent*

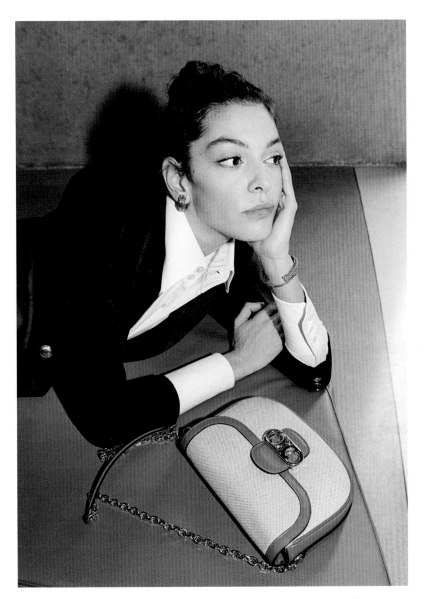

JACKET, SHIRT, EARRINGS and BRACELET by *Saint Laurent*, BAG by *Celine*

THIS PAGE: JUMPER by *Margaret Howell*, TROUSERS and BROOCH by *Patou*, EARRINGS by *Celine*

OPPOSITE: JACKET by *Scye*, JUMPER by *John Smedley*, T-SHIRT by *Trunk* from *Trunk Clothiers*, TROUSERS by *Scye Basics*

SHIRT, SKIRT, EARRINGS and NECKLACE by *Dior*

COAT by *Mackintosh*, JUMPER by *Norse Projects*, GLASSES by *Persol*

COAT by *Graphpaper*,
JUMPER by *Drake's*,
TROUSERS by *Loro Piana*,
SHOES by *A Kind of Guise*

—

HAIR AND MAKE-UP:
Yoana TG

—

MODELS: *Christopher Poulter
& Marta Ortiz*

—

LOCATION: *Centre National
de la Danse, Paris*

NOW OPEN IN HONG KONG AIRPORT

Stay informed and cosy on your next flight with a selection of print and plenty of other items at our shop in Hong Kong International Airport. Discover limited-edition collaborations and exclusive local products in our largest shop to date.

IN THE BAG

Look the business with a suit bag or neat travel tote, courtesy of our collaboration with Porter.

BEST READS

We stock a range of exceptional print titles, including our own magazines, travel guides and books.

LOOKING FINE

Pick up wrinkle-free Italian suits and cosy Japanese clothes; leave room for Portuguese swimwear too.

TRAVEL MUSTS

Stock up on stationery by Caran d'Ache and cute accessories by Delfonics, as well as travel essentials.

FIND OUT MORE: MONOCLE.COM/HKG

C'EST CHIC

Wendell Steavenson REPORTING FROM *Paris:* Overlooked for decades as French diners sought ever more outlandish haute cuisine, 'bouillons' are enjoying a revival. So what is so special about these bustling restaurants that serve simple homely food? We pull up a chair and take a bite.
PHOTOGRAPHER *Alex Cretey Systermans*

Bouillons predate the invention of the modern restaurant in the late 18th century – and the archaic venues are on the up again in Paris. Often set up next to butchers' shops, they were originally stalls that served soup based on a stock made from offcuts and bones. As restaurants diversified throughout the 19th and early 20th centuries – with some serving haute cuisine and others becoming brasseries or bistros – *bouillons* became popular everyday canteens. These vast, noisy, bustling places served simple, inexpensive food to everyone from Édith Piaf to the workmen digging the Métro. Between 1850 and 1950 there were hundreds in Paris and other French cities. Many were operated as chains – the original fast-food joints – reaping the benefits of economies of scale and speedy service. And today they're back.

Ten years ago only Chartier, in the 9th arrondissement, remained. As cavernous as a railway station, with nicotine-stained walls, brass luggage racks above the tables and tables cheek by jowl, it was a place where waiters in black waistcoats scribbled orders on paper tablecloths. The food was unremarkable but notable for its adherence to old-fashioned dishes, which included *carrotes rapées*, *frisée* salad with lardons, snails, Toulouse sausage with puréed potatoes and roast chicken with chips. It was a breath of fresh air when so many places had succumbed to trends: square plates, balsamic drizzles and burgers. Chartier was a throwback, a visit to a different century, as welcoming to Japanese tourists in search of authentic Paris as it was to students living in the quarter. It was the kind of place where the food didn't really matter; there were plenty of other things to talk about.

1

Christophe Joulie and his father, who own more than a dozen restaurants in Paris, bought Chartier in 2007. "Everyone expected us to turn it into a brasserie," says Joulie. For decades *bouillons* had been gradually upgraded and restyled from their humble roots into more upscale places. But Joulie and his father upped the ante, sped up the service and managed to get five seatings at a table a day rather than two. "We saved the *bouillon*," he says. "The *bouillon* is part of our patrimony." Chartier grew in popularity so much that there was a queue outside the door every lunchtime.

Then, in 2017, a rival, Bouillon Pigalle, opened in the city's red-light district. Bouillon Pigalle respects the tropes – waiters in waistcoats, long banquettes – but the decor is clean and crisp: racing stripe red and white. There are racks overhead but the hip Parisian crowd are more likely to stow motorcycle helmets or tote bags than a valise.

"We wanted to go back to the food of our grandmothers," says Bouillon Pigalle director Jean-Christophe Le Hô. The menu is nostalgic and homely: bone marrow and toast, *tête de veau*, navarin of lamb, *blanquette de veau*. Its chef recently won the prize awarded by the Association de Sauvegarde de L'Oeuf Mayonnaise (really) for the world's best egg mayonnaise. The plates – modern and red-rimmed – arrive in droves as groups order several starters to share, tapas-style.

Most of the main dishes at Bouillon Pigalle cost less than €10; a typical meal for one, including wine, can be covered by a €20 note. It was an instant hit when it opened and today a queue still stretches past the McDonald's next door. Le Hô says that the older people who dine here often thank him for bringing back dishes that have otherwise disappeared from restaurant menus. "This was the bourguignon we had when we were kids," they say. On Wednesday afternoons, when schools finish early, parents bring their children here – and in the evenings,

1

Previous spread:
1.
Chartier was the only 'bouillon' in Paris for years

This spread:
1.
Escargot at Chartier
2.
Waiter at Chartier
3.
Toilet break
4.
A glass of merlot costs less than a Coke
5.
Families, tourists, locals: everyone is welcome
6.
Waiters scribble the order on the paper tablecloth and tot up the bill at the end

2

young people celebrate birthdays. "Tables compete with each other to sing loudest," says Le Hô.

When we visit we're surrounded by a group, spread over several tables, celebrating a birthday. As the lights dim and the waiters bring out profiteroles with candles in them, strains of "Happy Birthday" fill the room. "Thierry!" shouts one customer as a latecomer arrives, trying to make themselves heard above the din. Thierry then holds out his arms as if to hug everyone there. Café chairs are shuffled, room is made; young women at an adjacent table wave before Thierry bows and takes his seat.

Bouillon Pigalle has the kind of noisy atmosphere that encourages people to talk to their fellow diners; it's the sort of place where a guest might send over a bottle of wine if someone is noticeably celebrating an

"It's popular because of the beauty of the place and, of course, because of the price point"

anniversary. It's also egalitarian: the menu is printed in nine languages. Once the restaurant even hosted a wedding reception for 60 people. The party didn't reserve tables, Le Hô tells us; instead they warned the restaurant in advance before showing up at 18.00, when there would definitely be room. Le Hô tells me that he once saw a man and woman on adjacent tables meet, flirt, leave together and then return to the restaurant as a couple a few days later.

The height of the *bouillon* movement came in the early 20th century. After the Second World War, the establishments gained a reputation for being a bit down at heel; tastes changed and all but Chartier turned to fancier fare. Now they are being turned back to *bouillons* again. For decades Julien on the Faubourg St Denis was an embarrassment; the extraordinary soaring art nouveau space was almost devoid of diners. It served plain steaks garnished with a 1970s-style tomato carved into a rose. Now under a new owner, it has been restored to its *bouillon* beginnings and, once again, it's doing a roaring trade. British designer John Whelan made his name updating the interiors of classic French brasseries. He says that when they scraped back more than a century of paint, they found the original shade. "It was this incredible bright sea-green," he says. "This really gave us the faux legitimacy, if you like, to repaint the restaurant that colour."

Bouillon Julien's interiors are enchanting: nymphs and goddesses appear to hold up the high ceiling of green stained glass, the floor is covered with daisy-patterned tiles, mirrored walls reflect each other and globe lights glow like miniature moons. So why were these cheap restaurants so opulently decorated? "In 1906, when Julien was opened, entertainment was the theatre and dining," says Whelan. "That's why you see these extravagant interiors in theatres, brasseries and *bouillons*. They were like the Hollywood blockbusters of their day."

The renewed popularity of the *bouillon* is growing. Joulie has turned a brasserie in Montparnasse, that was once a *bouillon*, back to its roots – and the team behind Bouillon Pigalle are planning to open another space in République. There are now also *bouillons* in Toulouse and Strasbourg, and even a joint venture between a Frenchman and a Czech in Prague called Le Petit Bouillon – a name that belies its size and grandeur.

For Whelan the reasons for the success of Bouillon Julien are obvious. "It's popular because of the beauty of the place and, of course, because of the price point," he says. "People come for family occasions because it feels grand and civilised and the young people come because they can afford it. There's a democratic vibe."

After decades of restaurants climbing higher and higher into the stratosphere of foamy, fussy haute cuisine, neighbourhood bistros have closed and the resurgence of the *bouillon* can be read as a down-to-earth reaction. Ask a French restaurateur what makes a good restaurant and they'll mention the ambience. In the rush to appease trends – fermented and foraged innovation, Asian flavours, clean eating – some have forgotten what the French always knew: the purpose of restaurants is less about the food and more about congregation, congress and company. Cheap and cheerful is the new fine dining. — (M)

1.
Bouillon Pigalle's menu is printed in nine languages
2.
Take a seat
3.
Ever-popular profiteroles
4.
Tables are tightly packed so neighbours often get talking
5.
Boeuf bourguignon and macaroni

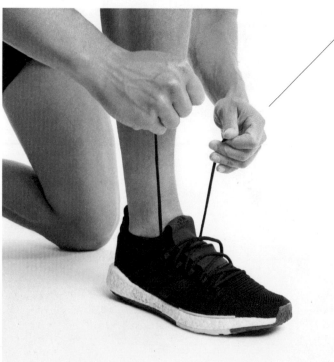

FRESH TAKES

Gain some new-year momentum by getting your hands on these latest life-enhancing goods – created by Monocle in collaboration with a selection of our favourite global brands.

From the buttons and buckles to the belts, braces and laces, we've got your 2020 look all tied up – just ask the Japanese wishing doll.

① MONOCHAN DARUMA by *Monocle* £22 ② FINE CORDUROY WORK JACKET by *De Bonne Facture* × *Monocle* £480 ③ PULSEBOOST TRAINERS HD by *Adidas* × *Monocle* £260 ④ MEDIUM SHOULDER BAG by *Archipel* × *Monocle* £330

These first-rate fragrances, grooming aids and travelling accessories are sure to present you in the best light possible.

⑤ LUGGAGE BELT WITH POUCH by *Johanna Gullichsen* × *Monocle* £95 ⑥ TOILETRY SET by *Farmers'* × *Monocle* £85 ⑦ BRASS OIL LAMP by *Karlskrona Lampfabrik* × *Monocle* £145 ⑧ SCENT FOUR: YOYOGI by *Comme des Garçons* × *Monocle* £80 ⑨ PVC POUCHES by *Delfonics* × *Monocle* £14–£35

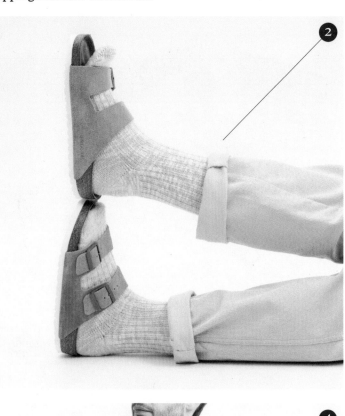

If you're hoping to see out the season in comfort, there's no reason why you shouldn't look your very best while doing so.

① SMALL SHOULDER BAG by *Archipel* × *Monocle* £260 ② ARIZONA SANDAL WITH SOCKS by *Birkenstock* × *Monocle* £190 ③ SHELL-JACKET WITH ZIP-IN GILET by *The Workers Club* × *Monocle* £750 ④ CASHMERE SHAWL CARDIGAN by *Iris von Arnim* × *Monocle* £765

Home or away, from desk to departure lounge, you need never surround yourself with anything that's less than exemplary.

(5) SEE-THROUGH TRAVEL TOILETRY POUCH by *R. Horn's* × *Monocle* £145 (6) SEAPLANE by *Mad Lab* × *Monocle* £95 (7) WEEKLY DIARY 2020 by *Mark's* × *Monocle* £25 (8) SMALL AND LARGE MUG SET by *Hasami* × *Monocle* £45 and £50 (9) GIRA DESK LAMP by *Santa & Cole* × *Monocle* £380 (10) RANGE OF BAGS by *Porter* × *Monocle* £260–£495

FROM THE GROUND UP

Josh Fehnert REPORTING FROM *Cork:* Irish TV chef and food writer Darina Allen has trained generations of chefs at her Ballymaloe cookery school but fears a loss of skills in the kitchen. She talks public health, the perils of oat milk and the agrarian revolution. PHOTOGRAPHER *Dan Wilton*

1

Has the farm-to-fork movement changed our attitude to waste and given us better food?
Sadly not enough has changed because the message nowadays is that academic skills are important but practical skills aren't. Big mistake. We've let at least two generations out of our houses and schools without equipping them with the life skills to feed themselves, which feeds right into the hands of the multinational food companies. We've handed over complete control over the most important thing in our lives really: our health. We're failing in our duty of care to our children and the next generation.

So teaching hands-on cookery skills and where our food comes from should be higher on the agenda?
I mean, I could be teaching algebra or geometry or something. And of course that's hugely important but you can't eat a flipping maths book. I feel fortunate that I've found something that I totally love doing and feel like jumping out of bed every day at 71 years of age. Maybe not quite as fast as I used to but still.

What's the first recipe that you share with students who attend your three-month certificate course at the cookery school?
Compost. I introduce them to the gardeners and the farm manager, and maybe I'll have a bunch of carrots or something. I say, "Look at these lovely carrots. It took Eileen the gardener three months to grow these carrots so don't you dare boil the hell out of them." We go out into the fruit garden and Eileen will have a wheelbarrow full of soil there. And actually it's humus [decaying soil]. They stand around me in a big semicircle wondering what's happening and feeling a little awkward. I run my hands through the soil and I say to them, "Remember, this is where it all starts." So they think I'm

For more than three decades Darina Allen has been tempting would-be chefs and curious food folk from around the world to a single bucolic corner of County Cork in her native Ireland. The lure? Her world-famous cookery school Ballymaloe, which has trained generations of international chefs and food entrepreneurs from home and abroad. Her mission? To change our relationship with food, farming and the land for the better, one step at a time.

Allen has written 19 cookbooks, made countless television shows and steered the course of international cookery away from trickery, fuss and foam towards fresh ingredients, time-honoured techniques and sensible farming practices.

Her enthusiasm is undimmed and she's got ideas – and answers – aplenty. Just don't offer her a skinny latte. — (M)

1.
Listen to 'The Big Interview' at monocle. com/radio for more from Darina Allen

> "The message now is that practical skills aren't important. Big mistake"

some aged hippie on a mission but I have to shock them out of thinking that food is something that comes wrapped in plastic off a supermarket shelf.

You've said elsewhere that you'd have liked to be a soil scientist. Why?
We're totally dependent on the health of four or five inches of soil around the world for our very existence. Farmers are really worried about the diminishing fertility of the land because we've wrecked the soil with very intensive monoculture over the years. We can't go on with business as usual – we have to go back. As a farmer I feel a strong responsibility to look somebody straight in the eye and know that that food is going to nourish them rather than make them ill, which is happening with a lot of food nowadays.

How has science helped us understand that relationship with food better?
There's been an enormous amount of work done on the link between the health of our gut and our mental and physical health – and that's obvious when you think of it. I've watched this over 30 years. For the past five, six, seven courses we've had at least one doctor, sometimes two; at the moment we have three doctors on the 12-week cooking course. These are medical professionals who tell me that they feel there isn't enough training in nutrition but who are now demanding the proper information so they can answer their patients' queries properly.

So many patients have conditions that can be at least helped, and often cured, by diet. But where do you get nutrient-dense food? A lot of people don't have time to buy directly from farmers but there are other ways and alternative routes to market. In the UK you have Farmdrop, where the growers get 80 per cent of their price, which is fantastic. So many farmers are not being paid enough to produce nourishing, wholesome food: just 30 to 40

> **"There is no such thing as cheap food in health terms nor socio-economic terms"**

per cent if it's sold through a supermarket. I'm always encouraging people to try to grow something themselves too.

How do you account for the rise in gluten and dairy alternatives?
There is so much misinformation. There is a sort of desperation and huge confusion. People are trying to make sense of all the different advice. There's such emphasis on the plant-based diet now but the real problem is the whole cheap-food policy. There's no such thing as cheap food. In health terms, in socioeconomic terms, it's a complete and absolute disaster. In Ireland, 46 per cent of all food that's bought in supermarkets is ultra-processed. We are destined to be the most obese country in Europe by 2030. Our health service can't cope until a huge amount of money is spent on getting the message across that we need to eat real food.

So are people unduly concerned?
People are not imagining the food intolerances and the allergies. People are not imagining that they feel bloated or get rashes, or whatever, after they eat a very squishy slice of bread. For the first three years of the school, which opened in 1983, I'd never heard of coeliac disease. If you're coeliac, you're coeliac; that's a disease and it's lifelong. But today I suppose a quarter or a third of all the students will say they have some kind of mild intolerance. By the end of the 12 weeks I guarantee that nobody will be dairy free or have a gluten intolerance. That's because they're eating 48-hour fermented sourdough bread. They have the choice to drink raw milk. They're eating a completely different kind of food and they cannot get over how different they feel. And so their big mission when they leave us [as either chefs or to their previous vocations] is to link in with local farmers. And, if they're starting a business, to try and develop a network of small producers to buy from.

No oat milk in that flat white then?
I just want whole milk, please. If you go in for a coffee you've got this big, long spiel: "Do you want soy milk, coconut milk?" No. Just the real deal. That's what we all need but it's so hard to find.

CRITICAL MASS

Restaurant openings can buoy neighbourhoods and help set a city's culinary agenda. As such we asked a few of our favourite food writers for the inside scoop on some of the launches to look out for in the year ahead. ILLUSTRATOR *Saki Obata*

1. —— **Helsinki** *by Mikko Takala* —— Less formal and fussy fare awaits diners in the Finnish capital but they shouldn't ignore one of Europe's finest restaurants. ——

The Helsinki food scene in 2020 will witness a shift away from fine dining towards a more casual style of cooking, even home-style dishes, as restaurants offer simple, no-nonsense servings at more affordable prices.

The New Nordic trend will continue but in a less dogmatic, more approachable style. This means that the restaurants will still focus on the provenance of their ingredients while taking inspiration from other cultures, as well as the Nordic styles of old.

A good example of this will be **Lucy in the Sky Restaurant**, my personal pick for 2020. Located in an enticing setting on top of a high-rise by the sea, it focuses on farm-to-table ingredients and wild herbs while drawing inspiration from Japan and Asia. Finnish and Japanese cuisine have many elements in common and the mix is set to be very interesting.

Visitors to Helsinki should try the **Palace Restaurant**. It is unapologetically fine dining and very pricey but it is one of the best European restaurants I have eaten in for years. I'd also recommend **Grön**, **Inari**, **Penélope** and **BasBas** for a more affordable and relaxed approach.

ABOUT THE CRITIC: Mikko Takala is a Finnish food writer and author. He contributes to various Finnish newspapers and magazines and has written several cookbooks and travel guides.

2. —— **Hong Kong** *by Janice Leung Hayes* —— The current volatility will impact on the city's hospitality scene but you just can't keep a good restaurant down. ——

Hospitality veterans in protest-hit Hong Kong are preparing for tough and uncertain times. But even as visitor numbers slump and some tables empty out, restaurateurs are putting on a brave face. What's more, a fair share of investors and chefs are pressing on with new openings – and in a rather big way.

A sizeable corner of Tsim Sha Tsui, the touristy and well-trodden waterfront district, has been reborn thanks to homegrown property developer New World – The Rosewood Hotel and K11 Musea mall are among the new openings here. Dining options in the area are numerous and will continue to increase well into 2020.

The most anticipated of these is **Bayfare Social**, a glamorous, Spanish-inspired food hall conceived by Parts and Labor Design. In the same area, fêted baker Dominique Ansel is slated to open patisserie **Dang Wen Li** which, judging by the name, is eyeing expansion in China.

Yenn Wong, CEO of hospitality group JIA, has a knack of introducing Hong Kong to rising stars such as Jason Atherton and Julien Royer. Due to celebrate a decade in business, she has picked Mirazur alumnus Ricardo Chaneton to lead her new contemporary French fine diner **Mono**.

Many of the city's best Cantonese restaurants are taking a more detailed look at the areas around the Pearl River Delta for niche ingredients and lost recipes. You'd do especially well to head to **The Chairman**, one of Hong Kong's most celebrated Cantonese restaurants. Its new menu features a specific breed of goose from the city of Foshan, roe from estuary crabs and house-pickled chillies inspired by village recipes.

The city's insatiable demand for meat was made embarrassingly clear when it was revealed during the Amazon fires that most of Brazil's beef exports end up in Hong Kong. Advocates for a more sustainable way of eating are now more active than ever, with chef and founder Peggy Chan leading the way. Fresh from opening her fine-dining vegan restaurant **Nectar** she is launching a cooking school called **Pollen Lab** to inspire diners to graduate from beef to beets. There's plenty to stew over in Hong Kong when it comes to politics; luckily, the food scene has provided us with lots to chew over too.

ABOUT THE CRITIC: For the past decade, Janice Leung Hayes has been a food critic and writer for publications such as the *South China Morning Post*, *Hong Kong Tatler* and *Travel + Leisure*.

3. —— Rachel Roddy's Rome

—— The Italian capital excels in getting the best out of the basics and an increasing number of innovative venues are happy to play on that. ——

Fifteen years after ending up in Rome on a whim, Rachel Roddy lives in the Testaccio district and has become an important culinary voice when it comes to Roman restaurants. She has a weekly column in *The Guardian* and several books under her belt.

This London-raised writer can be held partly responsible for elevating the understanding and appreciation of *la cucina romana* in the Anglosphere. Her tastes and talent as a cook and writer are linked to home cooking and simple grub; things with which Roman cuisine are synonymous. "In its body Rome is a big city but in its stomach it is a little village," says Roddy, describing the traditional rough-and-ready palate that dominates the Italian capital. It's hard, therefore, for her to talk of trends but the subtle evolution of the quintessential trattoria into something contemporary is exciting.

One such "neo-trattoria" is **SantoPalato**, where young head chef Sarah Cicolini is "going back to her Abruzzo roots while being fresh and playful", says Roddy. Here you'll find tripe (a Roman delicacy) but also braised peas with egg and parmesan – a riff on traditional pea and pasta soup. The proliferation of pizzerias in the city fascinates Roddy. "Pizza is an incredibly successful formula for eating out," she says, citing **180g Pizzeria Romana**, **Pizzarium Bonci** and **Trapizzino** as worthy of hype. "At heart, Rome's appetite is grounded in dough and tomato." — DMP

ABOUT THE CRITIC: Rachel Roddy's next book, *An A–Z of Pasta*, which she attests will be about "far more than pasta grannies", will be published by Penguin in 2020.

4. —— Amy Rosen's Toronto

—— The dynamism and diversity of Canada's largest metropolis are reflected in its slew of bold and forward-thinking establishments. ——

Unlike the spoiled residents of Rome or Paris, Toronto natives don't possess a storied culinary history or singular food stuffs that define their city. Instead its kitchens are propelled by youth and diversity: its residents come from more than 100 nations. "Borderless and unfussy, [Toronto is] young and free," says food critic Amy Rosen, summing up the state of the city's culinary scene.

"Casual settings with interesting wine cards that complement thoughtful shared plates are the common denominator," says Rosen of the restaurants setting themselves apart in Canada's largest city. She points to upscale French diner **Aloette** – the younger sibling of **Alo**, regularly cited as Canada's best restaurant – for its wedge salad and lemon meringue pie. At **Donna's**, a west-end snack bar helmed by a team of Momofuku veterans, "every table seems gifted with plump shrimp-salad sandwiches and ham-and-bread plates".

The culinary scene is shifting – but with change comes opportunity. "Toronto restaurants don't see it as a loss when forced to recalibrate," says Rosen. David Chang's Daisho and Shoto, for instance, have shut to give way to **Kojin**, Momofuku's wood-fired steak joint. "The Black Hoof, arguably the pivotal player in igniting Toronto's modern culinary scene a decade ago, has been reopened as **Bar Vendetta** by the same owners," says Rosen. "With youth comes courage." — WK

ABOUT THE CRITIC: Formerly the editor in chief of *Modern Farmer* and food editor at *Chatelaine*, Rosen also served as the first food critic for *EnRoute*, Air Canada's in-flight magazine.

5. —— *Sydney* by *Terry Durack*

—— Expect a celebration of excellent seafood on menus this year, while the city's nightlife is also set to get an overdue shot in the arm. ——

As the ongoing drought in New South Wales impacts on beef and lamb prices, restaurateurs are finding new ways to cope. Italian food, never far away, is a big growth area, thanks to its emphasis on pasta and pizza. Overall there's a shift to coastal cuisine, including new uses for seaweed, sea urchin and sea succulents, as well as a lot of fin-to-tail among chefs such as Josh Niland of **Saint Peter** and the **Fish Butchery**. If all you want to do in Sydney is eat simple fish and seafood next to the water, make for **Cirrus** at Barangaroo, the reinvented **Bathers' Pavilion** on Balmoral Beach or **Fred's** on Oxford Street in Paddington.

We're finally seeing Indigenous talent in our kitchens thanks to the National Indigenous Culinary Institute, which trains chefs with industry leaders such as Neil Perry of **Rockpool Bar & Grill**, and Guillaume Brahimi of **Bistro Guillaume**. I'm looking forward to **The Gidley**, a steak-and-martini concept from the team behind the very Florentine Bistecca. And it will be fascinating to see how Parramatta develops into a "second city", with chefs wondering whether to head to the western suburb.

As Sydney's barbaric licensing laws are finally repealed, **Mary's Underground** is ready with live music every night of the week, and the Prince of York has installed a perfectly pink basement bar called **Pamela's** with a permanently rotating disco ball.

ABOUT THE CRITIC: As chief restaurant critic for *The Sydney Morning Herald* and senior reviewer for the *Good Food Guide 2020*, Terry Durack knows his way around Sydney's dining scene.

MONOCLE 24: THE ENTREPRENEURS

Our weekly business show brings you insights from founders working in everything from retail to tech and explores the challenges involved in running a company or growing a brand. Hear what makes business leaders tick – and what keeps them awake at night.

'Based on everything I've heard, it's time to start a start-up'

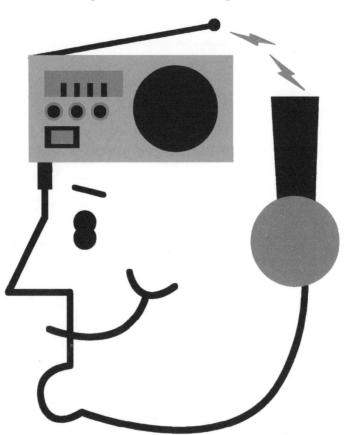

INSIDER INSIGHTS

Hear the brightest lights explain how to secure investment and manage growth.

EUREKA MOMENTS

Don't forget *The Entrepreneurs'* sister show *Eureka*, which tells the origin story of great brands.

GLOBAL COVERAGE

We cover a diverse range of businesses operating in cities and countries around the world.

SUCCESS STORY

Whether you already run your own business or really want to, this is the only programme you need.

LISTEN LIVE AT MONOCLE.COM OR SUBSCRIBE TO OUR PODCASTS; ALSO ON ITUNES, SPOTIFY AND ALL GOOD AUDIO PLATFORMS

BEST OF BOTH WORLDS

Fiona Wilson REPORTING FROM *Okinawa:* The Halekulani hotel is a dream destination for its Japanese guests, with just one drawback: it's in Honolulu. So the owners decided to reproduce its many charms in a paradisal landscape closer to home. **PHOTOGRAPHER** *Takafumi Matsumura*

Regular visitors to Honolulu will already be familiar with Halekulani, the legendary hotel whose own story is entwined with the birth and growth of Hawaiian tourism. Tucked among the crowded front row on Waikiki Beach, Halekulani, which translates as "House Befitting Heaven", opened in 1907 as a residential hotel. In the 1980s it was bought by Japanese property company Mitsui Fudosan, which remodelled the property. Today Halekulani is regularly voted the island's favourite hotel and 60 per cent of the clientele are Japanese.

Although many holiday-poor Japanese travellers are prepared to fly to the middle of the Pacific for a long weekend, it made sense for Mitsui to offer a second Halekulani experience closer to home – and Okinawa was the obvious location. Due to its subtropical climate, the promise of zero jetlag and easy three-hour flight from Tokyo, this archipelago off Japan's southern tip appeals to locals.

In 2015, Mitsui Fudosan acquired a prime beach property in Nago, in the north of the main island. "In terms of the view and location, we knew it would work for Halekulani," says Mitsui's project manager Yoshiaki Murata, who oversaw the 2019 opening.

The leisurely drive from the city of Naha, which hosts the nearest airport, allows about an hour to adjust to the warmth and pace of the island. The Ryukyu Kingdom, as Okinawa was once known, was proudly independent until Japan annexed it towards the end of the 19th century; it was ceded to the US after the Second World War and only reunited with the rest of Japan in 1972.

Today the culture is a beguiling mix of Okinawan and Japanese, with hints of Chinese and curious remnants of the US occupation, such as a love of spam (not shared by the rest of Japan) and a legacy of mid-century concrete military homes, which have been pleasingly weathered by fierce sun and humidity.

Nago is in pineapple territory. Turn left off Okinawa's one expressway and the lush vegetation reveals itself. Hotels are dotted around but few can claim such a spectacular perch (Halekulani lies within a national park). Architectural giant Nikken Sekkei designed the building: a long, slender structure that hugs the expansive coastline and gives everyone a sea view (something many Honolulu visitors can only dream of).

The interiors were created by multiple designers: New York studio Champalimaud Design conceived the guest rooms, lobby and two restaurants; LA-based Naoko Horii designed smart French restaurant Shiroux and Japanese restaurant Aomi; Belt Collins Hawaii took care of the landscaping.

"It wasn't a simple matter of replicating Halekulani in Honolulu," says Murata. "The point of the architecture and design was to create a new resort hotel for Okinawa while retaining some of the sensibility and atmosphere of the original. We wanted to express 'Halekulani-ness' through an Okinawan lens." The architecture references the location too. "We used Ryukyu limestone in the base of the building and *hana* blocks [decorative concrete squares] that are a distinctive feature of

Okinawa." The roof is the same brown as in Honolulu but here it was partially made with local *kawara* clay roof tiles.

The serene guest rooms take their cue from the original Halekulani's signature seven shades of white; it's a subtle canvas that offsets the iridescent blues of the ocean and greens of the garden. Some rooms look out on Mount Katsuu and the Motobu Peninsula; others over open sea. There are 360 rooms in total, including five private villas with their own plunge pools and natural hot springs. Beyond this, the hotel has a sizeable spa with a large onsen bath and five treatment rooms. There are also four outdoor pools spread around the hotel (plus one indoor pool) as well as a quiet sandy beach with loungers and a bathing area.

In the evening, diners can choose from four main restaurants and there's a sea-view bar where guests gather to watch the setting sun. Bar manager Hiroshi Imayasu has crafted a menu of classic and Okinawa-inspired cocktails for the hotel. They include Route 58 (named after the highway that meanders north to south through the island), made with pineapple-infused rum, coconut water, Okinawan *shikuwasa* citrus, mango purée and vanilla bitters.

In Aomi, the Japanese restaurant, Nago-born sushi chef Hiroyoshi Tamaki shows off Okinawa's seafood. Tamaki, who has returned from stints at some of the top

1

2

3

"It wasn't a simple matter of replicating Halekulani. We wanted to express it via an Okinawan lens"

4 5

restaurants in Osaka and Tokyo, prepares an outstanding dinner using local fish such as *makubu* (tuskfish) and mahi-mahi, served with a chilled saké. It's all rounded off with a sliver of confectionery from Jahana Kippan in Naha, which uses 300-year-old recipes to make sweet treats such as *toganzuke* (sweetened Okinawan winter melon).

With all this to keep guests entertained and fed, it might seem as if there's little incentive to leave the grounds. But general manager Jun Yoshie and his team have come up with a programme of excursions. They include a night-kayaking trip to see fireflies (Okinawa is home to half of Japan's 50 types of fireflies) and an introduction to Okinawan karate. In addition, anyone curious to know how it is that Okinawans have one of the highest life-expectancy rates in the world should enjoy an outing to renowned rural restaurant Café Garamanjaku, which serves the herbs, *goya* (bitter melon) and other local produce that are thought to be the key to Okinawan longevity.

Occupancy rates at Halekulani have been sky high from the opening day so the hotel has clearly found its audience (so far almost entirely Japanese). "We think that the set-up makes the most of the great location and character of the place," says Murata. "The detailed service is just as Japanese guests would expect too." — (M)
okinawa.halekulani.com

Previous page:
1.
Halekulani Okinawa's main pool
2.
Beach staff Yu Kawazoe (*on left*) and Mitsunori Harada

This spread:
1.
The hotel hugs the coast
2.
Indoor pool
3.
Activity attendant Mari Kajitani
4.
Bar manager Hiroshi Imayasu
5.
Naoko Saida, manager at Aomi
6.
Shiroux restaurant

6

1

2

SELF AWARENESS

James Chambers REPORTING FROM *Hong Kong:* As affluent modern travellers seek a boost for brain and body, hotels are now mindful of the wellness boom's potential. We find out how Asaya at Rosewood Hong Kong accommodates this feel-good factor. PHOTOGRAPHER *Jimi Chiu*

The recently opened Asaya, on the sixth and seventh floor of the Rosewood in Hong Kong, provides a comforting, nest-like feel. Its outdoor courtyard and pools, surrounded by high whitewashed walls, contribute to a sense of a sanctuary in the sky, bathed in natural light and hidden from the hectic city. Meanwhile the hotel's lap pool, bar and gym, connected to the wellness centre, offer endless harbour views.

Asaya's Tony Chi-designed treatment rooms, bathhouses and beauty salon, plus two self-contained suites isolated from the Rosewood's 413 rooms, reflect the importance of wellness to the high-end hospitality industry.

3

1.
Dockside view of
the Rosewood
2.
Pool sun loungers
3.
Asaya atelier

4.
Renaud Marin,
head chef at
Asaya Kitchen
5.
Marin's pan-fried
sea bream

There's even a health-focused restaurant: the Mediterranean and Japanese-inspired Asaya Kitchen, headed by chef Renaud Marin.

"We are invested in your lifestyle, not just the next hour of your life," says Erin MacNeil, Rosewood's director of wellness. The Canadian expat wants to dispel the "yoga and granola" view of the concept by making it more accessible. She says it incorporates everything that makes us feel better: "Do you eat? Sleep? That's wellness."

The extensive offerings at Asaya range from an elevated take on massage packages (including a library of oils) to intravenous drips and minor cosmetic surgery; there's expressive-arts therapy and consultations with the on-site naturopathic doctor. Your writer settles on 3D skin analysis and a men's "anti-vice" facial. The diagnosis: my skin's dehydrated. I must drink more water.

MacNeil arrived in Hong Kong last year from Rosewood's sister hotel in Beijing, where she was spa director. Whereas traditional spas have become transactional, wellness is more pervasive: packages have become programmes and the services permeate the rest of the hotel. As a result, taking responsibility for wellness across a hotel means liaising with other departments, from head chef to head of HR.

The wellness boom comes down to two main factors: affluence and technology. Access to more money means that people want to live the best life. Meanwhile, smartphones and the like are increasing mental stress and result in a need to switch off. Health-conscious consumers are a positive development for hotels: data shows that spa users tend to be high-spending guests. It seems wellness is becoming the hospitality industry's holy grail. — (M)

4

5

Here to stay
Anticipated openings around the world in 2020.

Next year's hotel-openings headlines will include the Nomad's London landing and Rosewood hitting São Paulo but there's a wealth of other openings to watch. Here's our overview of some more addresses that you'll want to check in to.

Castello di Reschio
Lisciano Niccone, Italy

Come summer the Bolza family will open a 36-room hotel in the 11th-century castle on their Umbrian estate. Beyond the historic fortress, the estate encompasses 50 farmhouses (some now holiday rentals), stables, vineyards and olive groves, as well as architect Benedikt Bolza's design studio. Bolza is working with local craftsmen to revamp the building, while food for the restaurants will be sourced from the estate's farm. "We make five different wines, olive oil and honey," says Bolza.
reschio.com

Cheval Blanc
Paris

LVMH's hotel collection, Cheval Blanc, opens its first Parisian property in spring. The hotel has 72 rooms and suites designed by Edouard François and Peter Marino. "With this view you can visit Paris in one glance," says Olivier Lefebvre, head of LVMH hotel activities. Guestrooms are set up like apartments and the penthouse suite has a pool and terrace overlooking the Eiffel Tower. "We also want to welcome Parisians," says Lefebvre, noting that the hotel will have a bar and two restaurants, one headed by Michelin-starred Arnaud Donckele.
chevalblanc.com

Villa Copenhagen
Copenhagen

In spring the Danish capital's former central post office will reopen as a 390-room hotel over the road from the Central Station and Tivoli Gardens. "The neo-Baroque building has been restored to appear exactly as it was at its inauguration in 1912 when the Danish postal service moved in," says Villa Copenhagen's general manager Peter Høgh Pedersen. "It remains a centre for communication; somewhere people connect in a historic setting."
villacph.com

Ace Hotel Kyoto
Kyoto

Ace Hotel's first Asian outpost has been designed in collaboration with long-time partner Commune Design and architect Kengo Kuma. The hotel will merge eastern and western influences when it opens in spring. It will be the centrepiece of the Shin-Puh-Kan Redevelopment Project that is revitalising the old Kyoto Central Telephone Exchange and will include a ground-floor marketplace, among other amenities.
acehotel.com

The Raffles
Bali

Following the restoration of two historic properties – the Raffles Europejski Warsaw and the recently reopened Raffles Singapore – the hotel company is opening in Bali. Located in Jimbaran Bay, the property will encompass a collection of villas with breathtaking ocean views. Over the next three years, Raffles Hotels & Resorts is looking to double its portfolio to 28 properties.
raffles.com

Hotel Magdalena
Austin, Texas

Austin is having a moment. Not only has Proper Hotels opened its doors but Hotel Magdalena by Liz Lambert's Bunkhouse Group will arrive in 2020. "The hotel, inspired by the 1960s and 1970s, is a love song to that part of Austin," says Lambert. Designed by architects Ted Flato and David Lake, the 89-room property is a stone's throw from Bunkhouse's other hotels: the San José, Saint Cecilia and Austin Motel.
bunkhousegroup.com

The future of hospitality
Three forward-thinking general managers share their insights and plans for 2020.

There are many changes afoot in the hospitality industry. Although apartment-sharing apps have been gaining ground, nothing beats the service and sense of place of a good hotel. Opening one is now about engaging with the community rather than creating an ivory tower of comforts removed from the neighbourhood. It's about the human touch, trained staff and good design. We speak to three general managers from around the world and ask what's on their agenda for 2020 – and how hotels are likely to evolve. — (M)

Downtown LA Proper Hotel
Los Angeles
GENERAL MANAGER: *Stephane Lacroix*

LA-based Frenchman Stephane Lacroix has lived in the US since 1994. He's worked in more than 11 hotels, from Hôtel de Paris in Monte-Carlo to Baccarat in New York. He now heads the Downtown LA Proper Hotel, opening in early 2020. — MSS

Why did you get into hospitality?
Growing up in France, I got used to good food and drink at an early age. I knew if I couldn't make it in sports, I'd

work in hospitality. There's an artistry and ceremony to it; it's a team effort.

How are you preparing for the launch of Downtown LA Proper?
The past year has been about building our team and ensuring our hotel caters to our guests, as well as the community. We've been knocking on doors and taking our neighbours out for coffee.

What sets the hotel apart?
A strong sense of identity. The building, dating from the 1920s, used to be a private club – we've kept the pool and basketball court and reinvented the spaces as guest suites. Our designer, Kelly Wearstler, knows the city well and looked to Downtown LA as her muse. We also partnered with a local F&B duo: Suzanne Goin and Caroline Styne. The area is one of those rare parts of LA where you can ditch the car and walk – and it has a great dining and cultural scene.

What constitutes good hospitality?
It should be genuine, welcoming and consistent. The focus should be on the comfort of the guests and a seamless experience from start to finish.

What are your plans for 2020?
Proper Hotels will have four hotels by the end of 2020: San Francisco, Santa Monica, Austin and Downtown LA. In 2021 we'll open our fifth in Portland. *properhotel.com*

City picks
Lacroix's essential LA stop-offs.

1. THE RESTAURANT: Enjoy Suzanne Goin's cooking at our hotel, with farmers' market-fresh ingredients. *properhotel.com; thelucquesgroup.com*

2. THE MUSEUMS: Moca, Lacma and The Broad put on amazing exhibitions all year round. *moca.org; lacma.org; thebroad.org*

3. THE FAIR: The second edition of Frieze Los Angeles will offer an amazing programme in February. *frieze.com/fairs/frieze-los-angeles*

4. THE EVENT: When the LA Lakers or LA Clippers play in the NBA championships next year, the Staples Center will be rocking. *staplescenter.com*

Paramount House Hotel
Sydney
GENERAL MANAGER: *Eden Elan*

Eden Elan began working for Russell Beard, Ping Jin Ng and Mark Dundon – the team behind Paramount House Hotel and Paramount Coffee Project, among others – as a waitress six years ago. Today she's the general manager of the 29-room Paramount that opened its doors in Sydney's eastern suburb of Surry Hills in 2018. — MSS

What does being a GM involve?
I love hospitality and enjoyed crossing over from restaurants to hotels. It's not so different: it's all about good service, being passionate about your industry and kind to your guests. As our hotel is small and independent, I do look after staffing and operations but find that my role is a bit more detail focused: I source new suppliers and make sure our guests feel at home.

What sets the Paramount House Hotel apart?
We're a small team so we've started collaborating with like-minded brands and companies to round out the experience. For example, we've teamed up with the China Heights Gallery round the corner to obtain the hotel's art installations and we've also partnered with the Golden Age Cinema and Bar in the building, which shows films in the former screening room of Australia's Paramount Pictures headquarters.

How do you engage with the neighbourhood?

We've only been in the building since 2018 but several other tenants already have an established following, such as the Paramount Coffee Project. We're able to tap into these communities so that guests come in and see a buzzing place full of local people. They feel part of the community and Sydney right away. This is the new landscape for hotels: finding a way to integrate into a neighbourhood.

What constitutes good hospitality?

The biggest thing is to pre-empt someone's needs – being able to give someone something they didn't even know they wanted is the key.

How are hotels changing?

We're moving away from a rigid structure and the old definition of luxury. People are looking for more local and community-based hotels with service that's more approachable. Creating a well-designed room isn't the hard part: having intuitive staff who care is much harder. A hotel stay is a personal, intimate experience, so creating a connection with people, by taking the time to get to know them, is invaluable. Our hotel was designed by Breathe architects to get better with age – the copper façade will gain a patina – and that's how we run the hotel. We want to improve with time. *paramounthousehotel.com*

City picks

"As licensing laws are beginning to relax," says Elan, "we'll be seeing a more vibrant nightlife in the city."

1. THE RESTAURANT: Cafe Paci, a pop-up by chef Pasi Petanen, has opened permanently in Newtown. *cafepaci.com.au*

2. THE BAR: Dear Sainte Éloise invites winemakers and young chefs to run the bar for a night. *dearsainteeloise.com*

3. THE SHOP: At Provider Store in Surry Hills, owner Tara Bennett makes most homewares herself. *providerstore.com.au*

4. THE GALLERY: Visit The White Rabbit for modern Chinese art. *jnprojects.net/white-rabbit-gallery*

 3

The Park Hyatt
Tokyo
GENERAL MANAGER: *Hervé Mazella*

Provence-born Hervé Mazella worked at various top hotels, including Grand Hyatt Hong Kong, before joining Park Hyatt Tokyo, one of the most admired hotels in the world, in 2012. He's been in his current role since 2016. — FW

What's the role of a GM?

A general manager brings energy and inspires positivity. It's important to be out and about on the property, meeting guests and the team – to feel the pulse. There is no bad day, even when things are busy and stressful. I often tell people coming into our industry that to do this job you need to think with your heart. You have to care about things and love people. Everyone plays a part in a hotel. At all levels we are here to serve with humility. For me, this job is a lifestyle.

What constitutes good hospitality?

At a simple level, good hospitality is attending to and exceeding needs. There shouldn't be any saying "no". Above all, guests need us to get the basics right. We aspire to provide comfortable bedding, a calm atmosphere, a simple lighting system, easy connectivity and good water pressure. We can make a long list. From the earliest *auberges* to the hotels of tomorrow, people want comfort, a place to feel welcome, good food and somewhere that gets the basics right.

What should no hotel be without?

A soul, a personality, an identity. You want to be able to walk into a hotel and feel something. Good service means being devoted to people and requires a great deal of passion, empathy, care, flexibility and attention to detail. Technology has changed the business but the rules of hospitality remain. The show must go on: shoes laced, ties straight, smile in place, grooming impeccable. It's like a performance, where each individual has a role to play. This ballet of doormen, receptionists, housekeepers, chefs and waiters is choreographed and runs like clockwork thanks to planning and care.

What does the future hold?

Some hotels try too hard and make things too complicated. Guests want us to understand what their needs are at that specific moment. Even if you profile guest preferences, people come to hotels at different points in their life and their preferences change. We're all evolving and the team should be mindful of that.

Are you getting excited about the Olympics?

Of course. It is a great event and opportunity for Tokyo and Japan. However, we have to bear in mind that it's three weeks out of 52. We've been operating for more than 25 years and we'll continue after the Olympics. *hyatt.com*

City picks

"Tokyo is in a constant state of change," says Mazella. "I like to get 'lost' and explore areas where you can learn about the local culture."

1. THE RESTAURANT: Robataya is like live entertainment as the chefs grill the ingredients you've chosen from what's on display. *roppongi-robataya.com*

2. THE BAR: New York Grill and Bar at Park Hyatt Tokyo on the 52nd floor has 360-degree floor-to-ceiling windows. There are live jazz performances every night. *restaurants.tokyo.park.hyatt.co.jp*

3. THE GALLERY: Scai The Bathhouse showcases the best of Tokyo's contemporary-art scene. *scaithebathhouse.com*

ON THE HORIZON

Whether you're looking for a smaller city to call home *(Bergen, pictured, could be the ticket)* or rethinking your business plans, MONOCLE's monthly magazines and seasonal newspapers have you covered for fresh ideas. Oh, and tune into Monocle 24 radio for news, analysis, insight and your soundtrack for the year ahead.
Head to *monocle.com* to find out more and thanks for your support.